William W. Wallace

Acts and Words of our Lord and Saviour Jesus Christ

William W. Wallace

Acts and Words of our Lord and Saviour Jesus Christ

ISBN/EAN: 9783337313876

Printed in Europe, USA, Canada, Australia, Japan

Cover: Foto ©Lupo / pixelio.de

More available books at **www.hansebooks.com**

The Acts and Words

—OF OUR—

LORD AND SAVIOUR, JESUS CHRIST.

Compiled From

The Revised Version of the New Testament,

—AND ARRANGED IN—

CHRONOLOGICAL ORDER.

(*i. e.*—His Utterances as Found in Matthew, Mark, Luke, John, Acts, and Revelation, are Blended Without Repetition.

PHILADELPHIA:

THE PRESBYTERIAN PUBLISHING COMPANY.

No. 1510 Chestnut Street.

1882.

" *Let these words sink into your ears.*"—Luke ix. 44.

PUBLISHERS' NOTE.

The object in thus culling out and arranging in the order of their occurrence (according to approved harmonies of the Gospels) the recorded acts and utterances of our Lord, as interspersed throughout the narrative in the New Testament, is to familiarize the reader with the events chronologically bringing them within the scope of easy memorizing, and in a convenient shape for a pocket companion reference.

W.

PHILADELPHIA, January 1, 1882.

B. C. 1. **THE ANNUNCIATION.—Nazareth.**

GABRIEL TO MARY AND JOSEPH.

Matt. i. 18–25. Luke i. 26–38.

J. C.   Birth of Jesus.—Bethlehem.—Luke ii. 4–20.

HIS ACTS. | ## HIS WORDS.

12. In the Temple.
Jerusalem
Luke ii. 42–51.

(The Doctors amazed at His understanding and answers.)

(*To His Mother.*)

(Grows in wisdom and stature.)

How is it that ye sought me? Wist ye not that I must be in my Father's House?

30. His Baptism.
The Jordan.
Matt. iii. 15.
Holy Spirit descends upon him.—Luke iii. 21–23.

(*To John.*)
Suffer it now: for thus it becometh us to fulfil all righteousness.

(*To Satan.*)
It is written, Man shall not live by bread alone, but by every word that proceedeth out of the mouth of God. Again it is written, Thou shalt not tempt the Lord thy God.

The Temptation.
Desert of Judea.
Matt. iv. 4–11.
Mark i. 13.
Luke iv. 2–13.

Get thee hence, Satan: for it is written, Thou shalt worship the Lord thy God, and him only shalt thou serve.

Jan.-Feb. Two of John's disciples, Andrew and John,
31. ask for his abode.
John i. 38–47.

What seek ye?
Come, and ye shall see.

To Simon Peter.

Thou art Simon, the son of John. Thou shalt be called Cephas (Peter).

To Philip.

Follow me.

Of Nathaniel.

Behold an Israelite indeed, in whom is no guile.

HIS ACTS.	HIS WORDS.
To Nathaniel. John i. 48-51.	Before Philip called thee when thou wast under the fig-tree, I saw thee, . . . because I said unto thee, I saw thee under the fig-tree, believest thou? Thou shalt see greater things than these. Verily, verily, I say unto you, Ye shall see the heaven opened and the angels of God ascending and descending upon the Son of man.
April J. C. 31. A marriage. Cana of Galilee *First Miracle.* Water turned into wine. John ii. 4-11.	(*To his Mother.*) Woman, what have I to do with thee? Mine hour is not yet come. (*To the servants.*) Fill the water pots with water. Draw out now and bear unto the Ruler of the feast.
Capernaum. Abides many days.	
Jerusalem. The Passover. The Temple. He expels the traders. John ii. 13-25.	Take these things hence; make not my Father's house a house of merchandise. Destroy this temple, and in three days I will raise it up.
To Nicodemus. The new birth. John iii. 1-21.	Verily, verily, I say unto thee, Except a man be born anew, he cannot see the Kingdom of God. . . . Verily, verily, I say unto thee, Except a man be born of water and the Spirit, he cannot enter into the kingdom of God. That which is born of the flesh is flesh; and that which is born of the Spirit is spirit. Marvel not that I said unto thee, Ye must be born anew. The wind bloweth where it listeth, and thou hear-

HIS WORDS.

est the voice thereof, but knowest not whence it cometh, and whither it goeth; so is every one that is born of the Spirit. . . Art thou the teacher of Israel, and understandest not these things? Verily, verily, I say unto thee, We speak that we do know, and bear witness of that we have seen; and ye receive not our witness. If I told you earthly things, and ye believe not, how shall ye believe, if I tell you heavenly things? And no man hath ascended into heaven, but he that descended out of heaven, even the Son of man, which is in heaven. And as Moses lifted up the serpent in the wilderness, even so must the Son of man be lifted up: that whosoever believeth may in him have eternal life.

For God so loved the world, that he gave his only begotten Son, that whosoever believeth on him should not perish, but have eternal life.

For God sent not the Son into the world to judge the world; but that the world should be saved through him.

He that believeth on him is not judged: he that believeth not hath been judged already, because he hath not believed on the name of the only begotten Son of God.

And this is the judgement, that the light is come into the world, and men loved the darkness rather than the light; for their works were evil.

For every one that doeth ill hateth the light, and cometh not to the light, lest his works should be reproved. But he that doeth the truth cometh to the light, that his works may be made manifest, that they have been wrought in God.

HIS ACTS.

(He tarries in Judea baptizing.)
J. C.
31.   Judea to Galilee
April Jacob's Well, Sychar.
Dec. Woman of Samaria.
John iv. 1-38.

(*To the Woman.*)
Give me to drink. . .

If thou knewest the gift of God, and who is it that saith to thee, Give me to drink, thou wouldest have asked of him, and he would have given thee living water. . . . .

Every one that drinketh of this water shall thirst again:

HIS WORDS.

but whosoever drinketh of the water that I shall give him shall never thirst, but the water that I shall give him shall become in him a well of water springing up unto eternal life. .

Go, call thy husband, and come hither. . . . .

Thou saidst well, I have no husband: for thou hast had five husbands; and he whom thou now hast is not thy husband: this hast thou said truly. . . . .

Woman, believe me, the hour cometh, when neither in this mountain, nor in Jerusalem, shall ye worship the Father.

Ye worship that which ye know not: we worship that which we know: for salvation is from the Jews.

But the hour cometh, and now is, when the true worshippers shall worship the Father in spirit and truth: for such doth the Father seek to be his worshippers.

God is a Spirit: and they that worship him must worship in spirit and truth. . . . .

(The woman saith, I know that Messiah cometh; Jesus saith, I that speak unto thee am he.)

(*To His Disciples.*)

I have meat to eat that ye know not. . . My meat is to do the will of him that sent me, and to accomplish his work. Say not ye, There are yet four months, and then cometh the harvest? behold, I say unto you, Lift up your eyes, and look on the fields, that they are white already unto harvest. He that reapeth receiveth wages, and gathereth fruit unto life eternal; that he that soweth and he that reapeth may rejoice together. For herein is the saying true, One soweth, and another reapeth. I sent you to reap that whereon ye have not labored: others have labored, and ye are entered into their labor.

HIS ACTS.

(He abides two days. Many Samaritans converted.)

Second Miracle.
Teaches in Galilee. Heals Nobleman's Son of Capernaum.
Matt. iv. 12-17.
Mark i. 14.
Luke iv. 14-15.
John iv. 43-54.

Except ye see signs and wonders, ye will in no wise believe.
Go thy way, thy Son liveth.

HIS ACTS.	HIS WORDS.
J. C. 32. Mar.-Apr. Nazareth. Matt. iv. 13. Luke iv. 14–30. *He is Rejected.*	(He reads Isaiah).

The Spirit of the Lord is upon me. Because he anointed me to preach good tidings to the poor. He hath sent me to proclaim release to the captives. And recovering of sight to the blind. To set at liberty them that are bruised. To proclaim the acceptable year of the Lord.

To-day hath this scripture been fulfilled in your ears.

Doubtless ye will say unto me this parable, Physician, heal thyself: whatsoever we have heard done at Capernaum, do also here in thine own country.

Verily, I say unto you, No prophet is acceptable in his own country. But of a truth I say unto you, There were many widows in Israel in the days of Elijah, when the heaven was shut up three years and six months, when there came a great famine over all the land; and unto none of them was Elijah sent, but only to Zarephath, in the land of Sidon, unto a woman that was a widow. And there were many lepers in Israel in the time of Elisha the prophet; and none of them was cleansed, but only Naaman the Syrian. . . .

Capernaum. Matt. iv. 17. Mark i. 15. Luke iv. 31.	The time is fulfilled, and the Kingdom of God is at hand: repent ye, and believe in the Gospel.
By the Sea of Galilee. To Simon and Andrew.	Put out a little from the land, (He preached to the multitude from the boat.)
Then Again to Simon	Put out into the deep, and let down your nets for a draught. .
Third Miracle. Disciples Alarmed at Miraculous Draught of Fishes. Matt. iv. 18–22. Mark i. 16–20. Luke v. 1–11.	Fear not. Come ye after me, and from henceforth I will make you fishers of men.
The Synagogue. Heals Demoniac. Mark i. 21–28. Luke iv. 33–37.	Hold thy peace, and come out of him.

HIS ACTS.	HIS WORDS.
J. C. Capernaum. At Peter's house. 32. Heals the Mother-in-law and many others, and casts out devils. Matt. viii. 14–17. Mark i. 29–34. Luke iv. 38–41.	He forbids the devils to reveal him.
In the Desert. Matt. iv. 23. Mark i. 35–39. Luke iv. 42–43.	(After praying.) Let us go elsewhere into the next towns, that I may preach there also: for to this end came I forth. I must preach the good tidings of the Kingdom of God.
Summer Galilee. Heals the Leper. 32. Matt. viii. 1–4. Mark i. 40–45. Luke v. 12–16.	I will, be thou clean; see thou tell no man, but go thy way, and show thyself to the priest, and offer for thy cleansing the gift that Moses commanded for a testimony unto them.
Capernaum. Heals a Paralytic. Matt. ix. 2-8. Mark ii. 1–12. Luke v. 17–26. Power to forgive sins.	Son, be of good cheer; thy sins are forgiven. . . Wherefore think ye evil in your hearts? for whether is easier to say, Thy sins are forgiven; or to say, Arise and walk? But that ye may know that the Son of Man hath power on earth to forgive sins. (To the sick man.) I say unto thee Arise, and take up thy bed, and go unto thy house.
He calls Matthew and eateth with Publicans and sinners. Matt. ix. 9. Mark ii. 14. Luke v. 27.	Follow me.
Pool of Bethesda. Heals the impotent man suffering 38 years. John. v. 1–15.	Wouldst thou be made whole? Arise, take up thy bed, and walk. . .

HIS WORDS.

Behold thou art made whole: sin no more, lest a worse thing befall thee.
(*To the Jews.*)—John v. 16–47.
. . . My Father worketh even until now, and I work. . . Verily, I say unto you, The Son can do nothing of himself, but what he seeth the Father doing: for what things soever he doeth, these the Son also doeth in like manner. For the Father loveth the Son, and sheweth him all things that himself doeth, and greater works than these will he shew him, that ye may marvel. For as the Father raiseth the dead and quickeneth them, even so the Son also quickeneth whom he will. For neither doth the Father judge any man, but he hath given all judgement unto the Son; that all may honor the Son, even as they honor the Father. He that honoreth not the Son honoreth not the Father which sent him. Verily, Verily I say unto you, He that heareth my word, and believeth him that sent me, hath eternal life, and cometh not into judgement, but hath passed out of death into life. Verily, verily, I say unto you, The hour cometh, and now is, when the dead shall hear the voice of the Son of God; and they that hear shall live. For as the Father hath life in himself, even so gave he to the Son also to have life in himself: and he gave him authority to execute judgement, because he is the Son of man. Marvel not at this: for the hour cometh, in which all that are in the tombs shall hear his voice, and shall come forth; they that have done good, unto the resurrection of life; and they that have done ill, unto the resurrection of judgement.

I can of myself do nothing: as I hear, I judge: and my judgement is righteous; because I seek not mine own will, but the will of him that hath sent me. If I bear witness of myself, my witness is not true. It is another that beareth witness of me; and I know that the witness which he witnesseth of me is true. Ye have sent unto John, and he hath borne witness unto the truth. But the witness which I receive is not from man: howbeit I say these things, that ye may be saved. He was the lamp that burneth and shineth, and ye were willing to rejoice for a season in his light. But the witness which I have is greater than that of John: for the works which the Father hath given me to accomplish, the very works that I do, bear witness of me, that the Father hath sent me. And the Father which sent me, he hath borne witness of me. Ye have neither heard his voice

HIS WORDS.

at any time, nor seen his form. And ye have not his word abiding in you: for whom he sent, him ye believe not. Ye search the scriptures, because ye think that in them ye have eternal life; and these are they which bear witness of me; and ye will not come to me, that ye may have life. I receive not glory from men. But I know you, that ye have not the love of God in yourselves. I am come in my Father's name, and ye receive me not: if another shall come in his own name, him ye will receive. How can ye believe, which receive glory one of another, and the glory that cometh from the only God ye seek not? Think not that I will accuse you, to the Father: there is one that accuseth you, even Moses, on whom ye have set your hope. For if ye believed Moses, ye would believe me; for he wrote of me. But if ye believe not his writings, how shall ye believe my words?

The Sabbath Question.
Disciples pluck corn.
Matt. xii. 1-8.
Mark ii. 23-28.
Luke vi. 1-5.

Have ye not read what David did when he was an hungered, and they that were with him, how he entered into the house of God, when Abiathar was High Priest, and did eat the shewbread, which it was not lawful for him to eat. Neither for them that were with him, but only for the priests? Or have you not read in the law, how that on the Sabbath day the priests in the temple profane the Sabbath and are guiltless? But I say unto you, that one greater than the temple is here. But if ye had known what this meaneth, I desire mercy, and not sacrifice, ye would not have condemned the guiltless.

The Sabbath was made for man, and not man for the Sabbath. For the Son of Man is lord of the Sabbath.

Galilee.
Heals the withered hand on the Sabbath.
Matt. xii. 9-14.
Mark iii. 1-6.
Luke vi. 6-11.

(*To the Man.*)
Rise up, and stand forth in the midst.

(*To Pharisees.*)
I ask you, Is it lawful on the Sabbath day to do good or to do harm, to save a life or to destroy it? What man shall there be of you, that shall have one sheep, and if this fall into a pit on the Sabbath day, will he not lay hold on it, and lift it out? How much, then, is a man of more value than a sheep! Wherefore it is lawful to do good on the Sabbath. (*To the man.*) Stretch forth thy hand.

HIS ACTS.	HIS WORDS.
Sea of Tiberias. Multitudes follow. Matt. xii. 15-21. Mark iii. 7-12. He had healed many, and crowds pressed to touch him. Mountain near Capernaum. Chooses the Twelve Apostles, Matt. v. 1. Mark iii. 13-19. Luke vi. 12-19. and delivers The Sermon on the Mount. Matt. v. 1. to vii. 29. Luke vi. 20-49.	(Let) a little boat wait (on me) because of the crowd, lest they should throng (me.) (*Matthew.*) Blessed are the poor in spirit, for theirs is the kingdom of heaven. Blessed are they that mourn, for they shall be comforted. Blessed are the meek, for they shall inherit the earth.

Blessed are they that hunger and thirst after righteousness: for they shall be filled.

Blessed are the merciful: for they shall obtain mercy.

Blessed are the pure in heart: for they shall see God.

Blessed are the peacemakers: for they shall be called sons of God.

Blessed are they that have been persecuted for righteousness' sake: for theirs is the kingdom of heaven. Blessed are ye when *men* shall reproach you and persecute you, and say all manner of evil against you falsely, for my sake. Rejoice, and be exceeding glad: for great is your reward in heaven: for so persecuted they the prophets which were before you.

Ye are the salt of the earth: but if the salt have lost its savour, wherewith shall it be salted? It is thenceforth good for nothing, but to be cast out and trodden under foot of men. Ye are the light of the world. A city set on a hill cannot be hid. Neither do *men* light a lamp, and put it under the bushel, but on the stand; and it shineth unto all that are in the house. Even so let your light shine before men, that they may see your good works, and glorify your Father which is in heaven.

Think not that I came to destroy the law or the prophets: I came not to destroy, but to fulfil. For verily I say unto you, Till heaven and earth pass away, one jot or one tittle shall in no wise pass away from the law, till all things be accomplished. Whosoever therefore shall break one of these least commandments, and shall teach men so, shall be called least in the kingdom of heaven: but whosoever shall do and teach them, he shall be called great in the kingdom of heaven. For I say unto

HIS WORDS.

you, that except your righteousness shall exceed *the righteousness* of the scribes and Pharisees, ye shall in no wise enter into the kingdom of heaven.

Ye have heard that it was said to them of old time, Thou shalt not kill; and whosoever shall kill shall be in danger of the judgement: but I say unto you, that every one who is angry with his brother shall be in danger of the judgement; and whosoever shall say to his brother, Raca, shall be in danger of the council; and whosoever shall say, Thou fool, shall be in danger of the hell of fire. If therefore thou art offering thy gift at the altar, and there rememberest that thy brother hath aught against thee, leave there thy gift before the altar, and go thy way, first be reconciled to thy brother, and then come and offer thy gift. Agree with thine adversary quickly, whiles thou art with him in the way; lest haply the adversary deliver thee to the judge, and the judge deliver thee to the officer, and thou be cast into prison. Verily I say unto thee, Thou shalt by no means come out thence, till thou have paid the last farthing.

Ye have heard that it was said, Thou shalt not commit adultery: but I say unto you, that every one that looketh on a woman to lust after her hath committed adultery with her already in his heart. And if thy right eye causeth thee to stumble, pluck it out, and cast it from thee: for it is profitable for thee that one of thy members should perish, and not thy whole body be cast into hell. And if thy right hand causeth thee to stumble, cut it off, and cast it from thee: for it is profitable for thee that one of thy members should perish, and not thy whole body go into hell. It was said also, Whosoever shall put away his wife, let him give her a writing of divorcement: but I say unto you, that every one that putteth away his wife, saving for the cause of fornication, maketh her an adulteress: and whosoever shall marry her when she is put away committeth adultery.

Again, ye have heard that it was said to them of old time, Thou shalt not forswear thyself, but shalt perform unto the Lord thine oaths: but I say unto you, Swear not at all; neither by the heaven, for it is the throne of God; nor by the earth, for it is the footstool of his feet; nor by Jerusalem, for it is the city of the great King. Neither shalt thou swear by thy head, for thou canst not make one hair white or black. But let your speech be, Yea, yea; Nay, nay: and whatsoever is more than these is of the evil *one*.

HIS WORDS.

Ye have heard that it was said, An eye for an eye, and a tooth for a tooth: but I say unto you, Resist not him that is evil: but whosoever smiteth thee on thy right cheek, turn to him the other also. And if any man would go to law with thee, and take away thy coat, let him have thy cloak also. And whosoever shall compel thee to go one mile, go with him twain. Give to him that asketh thee, and from him that would borrow of thee turn not thou away.

Ye have heard that it was said, Thou shalt love thy neighbor and hate thine enemy: but I say unto you, Love your enemies, and pray for them that persecute you; that ye may be sons of your Father which is in heaven: for he maketh his sun to rise on the evil and the good, and sendeth rain on the just and the unjust. For if ye love them that love you, what reward have ye? do not even the publicans the same? And if ye salute your brethren only, what do ye more *than others?* do not even the Gentiles the same? Ye therefore shall be perfect, as your heavenly Father is perfect.

Take heed that ye do not your righteousness before men, to be seen of them: else ye have no reward with your Father which is in heaven.

When therefore thou doest alms, sound not a trumpet before thee, as the hypocrites do in the synagogues and in the streets, that they may have glory of men. Verily, I say unto you, They have received their reward. But when thou doest alms, let not thy left hand know what thy right hand doeth: that thine alms may be in secret: and thy Father which seeth in secret shall recompense thee.

And when ye pray, ye shall not be as the hypocrites: for they love to stand and pray in the synagogues and in the corners of the streets, that they may be seen of men. Verily, I say unto you, They have received their reward. But thou, when thou prayest, enter into thine inner chamber, and having shut thy door, pray to thy Father which is in secret, and thy Father which seeth in secret shall recompense thee. And in praying use not vain repetitions, as the Gentiles do: for they think that they shall be heard for their much speaking. Be not therefore like unto them: for your Father knoweth what things ye have need of, before ye ask him. After this manner therefore pray ye: Our Father which art in heaven, Hallowed be thy name. Thy kingdom come. Thy will be done, as in heaven, so on

HIS WORDS.

earth. Give us this day our daily bread. And forgive us our debts as we also have forgiven our debtors. And bring us not into temptation, but deliver us from the evil *one*. For if ye forgive men their trespasses, your heavenly Father will also forgive you. But if ye forgive not men their trespasses, neither will your Father forgive your trespasses.

Moreover, when ye fast, be not, as the hypocrites, of a sad countenance: for they disfigure their faces, that they may be seen of men to fast. Verily, I say unto you, They have received their reward. But thou, when thou fastest, anoint thy head, and wash thy face; that thou be not seen of men to fast, but of thy Father which is in secret: and thy Father which seeth in secret shall recompense thee.

Lay not up for yourselves treasures upon the earth, where moth and rust doth consume, and where thieves break through and steal: but lay up for yourselves treasures in heaven, where neither moth nor rust doth consume, and where thieves do not break through nor steal: for where thy treasure is, there will thy heart be also. The lamp of the body is the eye: if therefore thine eye be single, thy whole body shall be full of light. But if thine eye be evil, thy whole body shall be full of darkness. If therefore the light that is in thee be darkness, how great is the darkness! No man can serve two masters: for either he will hate the one and love the other; or else he will hold to one, and despise the other. Ye cannot serve God and mammon. Therefore I say unto you, Be not anxious for your life, what ye shall eat or what ye shall drink; nor yet for your body, what ye shall put on. Is not the life more than the food, and the body than the raiment? Behold the birds of the heaven, that they sow not, neither do they reap nor gather into barns; and your heavenly Father feedeth them. Are not ye of much more value than they? And which of you by being anxious can add one cubit to his stature? And why are ye anxious concerning raiment? Consider the lilies of the field, how they grow; they toil not, neither do they spin: yet I say unto you, that even Solomon in all his glory was not arrayed like one of these. But if God doth so clothe the grass of the field, which to-day is, and to-morrow is cast into the oven, *shall he* not much more *clothe* you, O ye of little faith? Be not therefore anxious, saying, What shall we eat? or, What shall we drink? or, Wherewithal shall we be clothed? For after all these things do the Gentiles

HIS WORDS.

seek; for your heavenly Father knoweth that ye have need of all these things. But seek ye first his kingdom, and his righteousness; and all these things shall be added unto you. Be not therefore anxious for the morrow: for the morrow will be anxious for itself. Sufficient unto the day is the evil thereof.

Judge not, that ye be not judged. For with what judgement ye judge, ye shall be judged: and with what measure ye mete, it shall be measured unto you. And why beholdest thou the mote that is in thy brother's eye, but considerest not the beam that is in thine own eye? Or how wilt thou say to thy brother, Let me cast out the mote out of thine eye; and lo, the beam is in thine own eye? Thou hypocrite, cast out first the beam out of thine own eye; and then shalt thou see clearly to cast out the mote out of thy brother's eye.

Give not that which is holy unto the dogs, neither cast your pearls before the swine, lest haply they trample them under their feet, and turn and rend you.

Ask, and it shall be given you; seek, and ye shall find; knock, and it shall be opened unto you: for every one that asketh receiveth; and he that seeketh findeth; and to him that knocketh it shall be opened. Or what man is there of you, who, if his son shall ask him for a loaf, will give him a stone; or if he shall ask for a fish, will give him a serpent? If ye then, being evil, know how to give good gifts unto your children, how much more shall your Father which is in heaven give good things to them that ask him? All things therefore whatsoever ye would that men should do unto you, even so do ye also unto them: for this is the law and the prophets.

Enter ye in by the narrow gate: for wide is the gate, and broad is the way that leadeth to destruction, and many be they that enter in thereby. For narrow is the gate, and straitened the way, that leadeth unto life, and few be they that find it.

Beware of false prophets, which come to you in sheep's clothing, but inwardly are ravening wolves. By their fruits ye shall know them. Do *men* gather grapes of thorns, or figs of thistles? Even so every good tree bringeth forth good fruit; but the corrupt tree bringeth forth evil fruit. A good tree cannot bring forth evil fruit, neither can a corrupt tree bring forth good fruit. Every tree that bringeth not forth good fruit is hewn down, and cast into the fire. Therefore by their fruits ye shall know them. (Luke) But woe unto you that are rich! for ye have received your

HIS WORDS.

consolation. Woe unto you, ye that are full now! for ye shall hunger. Woe *unto you*, ye that laugh now! for ye shall mourn and weep. Woe *unto you*, when all men shall speak well of you! for in the same manner did their fathers to the false prophets. . . .

Can the blind guide the blind? shall they not both fall into a pit? The disciple is not above his master: but every one when he is perfected shall be as his master. . . The good man out of the good treasure of his heart bringeth forth that which is good; and the evil *man* out of the evil *treasure* bringeth forth that which is evil: for out of the abundance of the heart his mouth speaketh. And why call ye me Lord, Lord, and do not the things which I say?
(Matthew.)

Not every one that saith unto me, Lord, Lord, shall enter into the kingdom of heaven; but he that doeth the will of my Father which is in heaven. Many will say to me in that day, Lord, Lord, did we not prophesy by thy name, and by thy name cast out devils, and by thy name do many mighty works? And then will I profess unto them, I never knew you: depart from me, ye that work iniquity. Every one therefore which heareth these words of mine, and doeth them, shall be likened unto a wise man, which built his house upon the rock: and the rain descended, and the floods came, and the winds blew, and beat upon that house; and it fell not: for it was founded upon the rock. And every one that heareth these words of mine, and doeth them not, shall be likened unto a foolish man, which built his house upon the sand: and the rain descended, and the floods came, and the winds blew, and smote upon that house; and it fell: and great was the fall thereof.

HIS ACTS.

J. C. 32. Summer.

Capernaum.
Heals Centurion's Servant.
Matt. viii. 5-17.
Luke vii. 1-10.

I will come and heal him. Verily, I say unto you, I have not found so great faith, no, not in Israel: and I say unto you, that many shall come from the East and the West, and shall sit down with Abraham and Isaac and Jacob in the kingdom of heaven: but the sons of the

HIS ACTS.

Nain.
Raises the widow's Son. from the dead.
Luke vii. 11-17.
Disciples from John the Baptist in Prison.
Matt. xi. 2-30.
Luke vii. 18-35.

HIS WORDS.

kingdom shall be cast forth into the outer darkness: there shall be the weeping and gnashing of teeth. . . (To the Centurion.)
Go thy way: as thou hast believed, so be it done unto thee.
(*To the Mother.*)
Weep not.
(*To the Corpse.*)
Young man, I say unto thee, Arise.
Go your way, and tell John the things which ye do hear and see: the blind receive their sight, and the lame walk, the lepers are cleansed, and the deaf hear, and the dead are raised up, and the poor have good tidings preached to them. And blessed is he, whosoever shall find none occasion of stumbling in me.
(*To the Multitudes.*)
What went ye out into the wilderness to behold? a reed shaken with the wind? But what went ye out to see? a man clothed in soft *raiment?* Behold, they which are gorgeously apparelled, and live delicately, are in kings' houses. But wherefore went ye out? to see a prophet? Yea, I say unto you, and much more than a prophet. This is he, of whom it is written, Behold, I send my messenger before thy face, who shall prepare thy way before thee.
Verily, I say unto you, Among them that are born of women there hath not arisen a greater than John the Baptist: yet he that is but little in the kingdom of heaven is greater than he. And from the days of John the Baptist until now the kingdom of heaven suffereth violence, and men of violence take it by force. For all the prophets and the law prophesied until John. And if ye are willing to receive *it*, this is Elijah, which is come. He that hath ears to hear, let him hear. But whereunto shall I liken this generation? It is like unto children sitting in the marketplaces, which call unto their fellows, and say, We piped unto you, and ye did not dance; we wailed, and ye did not mourn. For John came eating no bread, nor drinking wine, and they say, He hath a devil. The Son of man is come eating and drinking, and ye say, Behold, a gluttonous man, and a wine-

HIS WORDS.

bibber, a friend of publicans and sinners! And wisdom is justified by her works. (Of all her children.—Luke.) . . .

Woe unto thee, Chorazin! woe unto thee, Bethsaida! for if the mighty works had been done in Tyre and Sidon which were done in you, they would have repented long ago in sackcloth and ashes. Howbeit I say unto you, it shall be more tolerable for Tyre and Sidon in the day of judgement, than for you. And thou, Capernaum, shalt thou be exalted unto heaven? thou shalt go down unto Hades: for if the mighty works had been done in Sodom which were done in thee, it would have remained until this day. Howbeit I say unto you, that it shall be more tolerable for the land of Sodom in the day of judgement, than for thee. . .

. . I thank thee, O Father, Lord of heaven and earth, that thou didst hide these things from the wise and understanding, and didst reveal them unto babes: yea, Father, for so it was well pleasing in thy sight. All things have been delivered unto me of my Father: and no one knoweth the Son, save the Father; neither doth any know the Father, save the Son, and he to whomsoever the Son willeth to reveal *him*. Come unto me, all ye that labor and are heavy laden, and I will give you rest. Take my yoke upon you, and learn of me; for I am meek and lowly in heart: and ye shall find rest unto your souls. For my yoke is easy, and my burden is light.

HIS ACTS.

J. C.
Midsummer.
32.

Capernaum.
Eats with Simon (a Pharisee.)
Woman with alabaster box of ointment.
Luke vii. 37-50.
Rebukes Simon, and forgiveth her sins.

Simon, I have somewhat to say unto thee. A certain lender had two debtors: the one owed five hundred pence, and the other fifty. When they had not *wherewith* to pay, he forgave them both. Which of them therefore will love him most? (Simon said, He to whom he forgave the most.) Thou hast rightly judged. (Turning to the woman.) Seest thou this woman? I entered into thine house, thou gavest me no water for my feet: but she hath wetted my feet with her tears, and wiped them with her hair. Thou gavest me no kiss: but she, since the time I came in, hath not ceased to kiss my feet. My head with oil thou didst not

HIS WORDS.

anoint: but she hath anointed my feet with ointment. Wherefore I say unto thee, her sins, which are many, are forgiven; for she loved much: but to whom little is forgiven, *the same* loveth little. (He said unto her,) Thy sins are forgiven. . . Thy faith hath saved thee: go in peace.

HIS ACTS.

J. C. Galilee.
Autumn. With the twelve he takes a second circuit.
32. Luke viii. 1.
Heals a blind and dumb Demoniac, Pharisees blasphemously ascribe his power to Beelzebub.
Matt. xii. 22-50.
Mark iii. 19-35.
Luke xi. 14-36.

How can Satan cast out Satan? Every kingdom divided against itself is brought to desolation: and every city or house divided against itself shall not stand: and if Satan casteth out Satan, he is divided against himself; how then shall his kingdom stand? And if I by Beelzebub cast out devils, by whom do your sons cast them out? therefore shall they be your judges. But if I by the Spirit of God cast out devils, then is the kingdom of God come upon you. Or how can one enter into the house of the strong *man*, and spoil his goods, except he first bind the strong *man?* and then he will spoil his house. He that is not with me is against me; and he that gathereth not with me scattereth. Therefore I say unto you, Every sin and blasphemy shall be forgiven unto men; but the blasphemy against the Spirit shall not be forgiven. And whosoever shall speak a word against the Son of man, it shall be forgiven him; but whosoever shall speak against the Holy Spirit, it shall not be forgiven him, neither in this world, nor in that which is to come. Either make the tree good, and its fruit good; or make the tree corrupt, and its fruit corrupt: for the tree is known by its fruit. Ye offspring of vipers, how can ye, being evil, speak good things? for out of the abundance of the heart the mouth speaketh. The good man out of his good treasure bringeth forth good things: and the evil man out of his evil treasure bringeth forth evil things. And I say unto you, that every idle word that men shall speak, they shall give account thereof in the day of judgement. For by thy words thou shalt be justified, and by thy words thou shalt be condemned. . . .

An evil and adulterous generation seeketh after a sign; and there shall no sign be given to it but the sign of Jonah the

HIS WORDS.

prophet: for as Jonah was three days and three nights in the belly of the whale, so shall the Son of man be three days and three nights in the heart of the earth. The men of Nineveh shall stand up in the judgement with this generation, and shall condemn it: for they repented at the preaching of Jonah; and behold, a greater than Jonah is here. The queen of the south shall rise up in the judgement with this generation, and shall condemn it: for she came from the ends of the earth to hear the wisdom of Solomon; and behold, a greater than Solomon is here. But the unclean spirit, when he is gone out of the man, passeth through waterless places, seeking rest, and findeth it not. Then he saith, I will return into my house whence I came out; and when he is come, he findeth it empty, swept, and garnished. Then goeth he, and taketh with himself seven other spirits more evil than himself, and they enter in and dwell there: and the last state of that man becometh worse than the first. Even so shall it be also unto this evil generation.
(*Luke.*)

No man, when he hath lighted a lamp, putteth it in a cellar, neither under the bushel, but on the stand, that they which enter in may see the light. The lamp of thy body is thine eye: when thine eye is single, thy whole body also is full of light; but when it is evil, thy body also is full of darkness. Look therefore whether the light that is in thee be not darkness. If therefore thy whole body be full of light, having no part dark, it shall be wholly full of light, as when the lamp with its bright shining doth give thee light.

HIS ACTS.

J. C.	They seek a sign.	
32.	A Woman Blesses Him.	Yea rather, blessed are they that hear the word of God and keep it.
	His mother and brethren are those who do the will of God.	Who is my mother? and who are my brethren? . . Behold, my mother and my brethren! For whosoever shall do the will of my Father which is in heaven, he is my brother, and sister, and mother.

HIS ACTS.

Matt. xiii. 1-53.
Mark iv. 1-34.
Luke viii. 4-18.
Parables.
By the Sea Side.
The Sower.
The Tares.
The Mustard Seeds.
The Leaven.
Treasure Hidden.
The Pearl.
The Net.
The Lamp.

HIS WORDS.

Hearken:—Behold, the sower went forth to sow; and as he sowed, some *seeds* fell by the way side, and it was trodden under foot, and the birds came and devoured them: and others fell upon rocky places, where they had not much earth: and straightway they sprang up, because they had no deepness of earth: and when the sun was risen, they were scorched; and because they had no root, they withered away. And others fell upon the thorns; and the thorns grew up, and choked them; and others fell upon the good ground, and yielded fruit, some a hundredfold, some sixty, some thirty. He that hath ears to hear, let him hear.
(*To the Disciples.*)
Unto you it is given to know the mysteries of the kingdom of heaven, but to them it is not given. For whosoever hath, to him shall be given, and he shall have abundance: but whosoever hath not, from him shall be taken away, even that which he hath. Therefore speak I to them in parables; because seeing they see not, and hearing they hear not, neither do they understand. And unto them is fulfilled the prophecy of Isaiah, which saith,
  By hearing ye shall hear, and shall in no wise understand;
  And seeing ye shall see, and shall in no wise perceive:
  For this people's heart is waxed gross,
  And their ears are dull of hearing,
  And their eyes they have closed;
  Lest haply they should perceive with their eyes,
  And hear with their ears,
  And understand with their heart,
  And should turn again,
  And I should heal them.
But blessed are your eyes, for they see; and your ears, for they hear. For verily I say unto you, that many prophets and righteous men desired to see the things which ye see, and saw them not; and to hear the things which ye hear, and heard them not. Hear then ye the parable of the sower. The seed is the word of God. When any one heareth the word of the kingdom, and understandeth it not, *then* cometh the evil *one*, and snatcheth

HIS WORDS

away that which hath been sown in his heart. that he may not believe and be saved. This is he that was sown by the way side. And he that was sown upon the rocky places, this is he that heareth the word, and straightway with joy receiveth it; yet hath he not root in himself, but endureth for a while; and when tribulation or persecution ariseth because of the word, straightway he stumbleth. And he that was sown among the thorns, this is he that heareth the word; and the care of the world, and the deceitfulness of riches, and pleasures of this life, choke the word, and he becometh unfruitful. And he that was sown upon the good ground, this is he that in an honest and good heart heareth the word, understandeth it, and holds it fast: who verily beareth fruit with patience, and bringeth forth, some a hundredfold, some sixty, some thirty.

(Another parable.) The kingdom of heaven is likened unto a man that sowed good seed in his field, but while men slept, his enemy came and sowed tares also among the wheat, and went away. But when the blade sprang up, and brought forth fruit, then appeared the tares also. And the servants of the householder came and said unto him, Sir, didst thou not sow good seed in thy field? whence then hath it tares? And he said unto them, An enemy hath done this. And the servants say unto him, Wilt thou then that we go and gather them up? But he saith, Nay, lest haply while ye gather up the tares, ye root up the wheat with them. Let both grow together until the harvest, and in the time of the harvest I will say to the reapers, Gather up first the tares, and bind them in bundles to burn them, but gather the wheat into my barn.

The kingdom of heaven is like unto a grain of mustard seed, which a man took and sowed in his field, which indeed is less than all seeds: but when it is grown, it is greater than the herbs, and becometh a tree, so that the birds of the heaven come and lodge in the branches, under the shadow thereof.

The kingdom of heaven is like unto leaven, which a woman took, and hid in three measures of meal, till it was all leavened.

To His Disciples.)

He that soweth the good seed is the Son of man; and the field is the world; and the good seed, these are the sons of the kingdom; and the tares are the sons of the evil *one;* and the enemy that sowed them is the devil; and the harvest is the end of the world; and the reapers are angels. As therefore the

HIS WORDS.

tares are gathered up and burned with fire, so shall it be in the end of the world. The Son of man shall send forth his angels, and they shall gather out of his kingdom all things that cause stumbling, and them that do iniquity, and shall cast them into the furnace of fire; there shall be weeping and gnashing of teeth. Then shall the righteous shine forth as the sun in the kingdom of their Father. He that hath ears, let him hear.

The kingdom of heaven is like unto a treasure hidden in the field; which a man found, and hid, and in his joy he goeth and selleth all that he hath, and buyeth that field.

Again, the kingdom of heaven is like unto a man that is a merchant seeking goodly pearls: and having found one pearl of great price, he went and sold all that he had, and bought it.

Again, the kingdom of heaven is like unto a net, that was cas into the sea, and gathered of every kind: which, when it was filled, they drew up on the beach; and they sat down, and gathered the good into vessels, but the bad they cast away So shall it be in the end of the world: the angels shall come forth, and sever the wicked from among the righteous, and shall cast them into the furnace of fire: there shall be the weeping and the gnashing of teeth.

Have ye understood all these things? . . . Therefore every scribe who hath been made a disciple to the kingdom of heaven is like unto a man that is a householder, which bringeth forth out of his treasure things new and old.

(*Mark and Luke.*)

And no man, when he hath lighted a lamp, covereth it with a vessel, or putteth it under a bed; but putteth it on a stand, that they which enter in may see the light. For nothing is hid, that shall not be made manifest; nor *any thing* secret, that shall not be known and come to light.

If any man hath ears to hear, let him hear. . . . Take heed what ye hear: with what measure ye mete it shall be measured unto you: and more shall be given unto you. For he that hath, to him shall be given: and he that hath not, from him shall be taken away, even that which he thinketh he hath.

So is the kingdom of God, as if a man should cast seed upon the earth; and should sleep and rise night and day, and the seed should spring up and grow, he knoweth not how. The earth beareth fruit of herself; first the blade, then the ear, then the

HIS WORDS.

full corn in the ear. But when the fruit is ripe, straightway he putteth forth the sickle, because the harvest is come.

HIS ACTS.

Galilee.

The foxes have holes and the birds of the heaven have nests: but the Son of man hath not where to lay his head.

Follow me: and leave the dead to bury their own dead; but go thou and publish abroad the kingdom of God.

No man having put his hand to the plow, and looking back, is fit for the kingdom of God.

Crossing the Lake, he fell asleep. Awakes and stills the tempest.
Visits Decapolis.
Matt. viii. 18–27.
Mark iv. 35–41.
Luke viii. 22–25.
Luke ix. 57–62.

Let us go over unto the other side of the lake.
Why are ye fearful, O ye of little faith? have ye not yet faith? (*To the Tempest.*)
Peace, be still.

Gadara.
Casts the devils out of the Demoniac, and they ask to enter the swine.
Matt. viii. 28–34.
Mark v. 1–20.
Luke viii. 26–39.

(The Gadarenes reject him.)

Come forth thou unclean spirit, out of the man. What is thy name?
Go (into the swine.)
(*To the Man.*)
Go to thy house unto thy friends, and tell them how great things the Lord hath done for thee, and how he had mercy on thee.

Capernaum.
Levi's Feast.
Matt. ix. 10–17.
Mark ii. 15–22.
Luke v. 28–39.

They that are whole have no need of a physician, but they that are sick. But go ye and learn what *this* meaneth, I desire mercy, and not sacrifice: for I came not to call the righteous, but sinners to repentance. . .

Can the sons of the bridechamber mourn, as long as the bridegroom is with them? but the days will come, when the bridegroom shall be taken away from them, and then will they

HIS WORDS.

fast. And no man putteth a piece of undressed cloth upon an old garment; for that which should fill it up taketh from the garment, and a worse rent is made. Neither do *men* put new wine into old wine-skins: else the skins burst, and the wine is spilled, and the skins perish: but they put new wine into fresh wine-skins, and both are preserved.

HIS ACTS.

Jairus' Daughter raised. A woman healed. Also two blind men, and devil cast out of a dumb man.
  Matt. ix. 18-31.
  Mark v. 22-43.
  Luke viii. 41-56.

Who is it that touched my garment? Some one did touch me: for I perceived that power had gone forth from me.
(*To the Woman.*)
Daughter, be of good cheer: thy faith hath made thee whole: go in peace.
(*To Jairus.*)
Fear not: only believe, and she shall be made whole.
Give place. Weep not: for the damsel is not dead, but sleepeth.
Maiden, arise! (Let) something be given her to eat.
Tell no man (of this).
(*To Blind Men.*)
Believe ye that I am able to do this? . . . According to your faith be it done unto you.
. . . . . .
See that no man know it. . .

(Goes about preaching and healing.)
Nazareth.
  Matt. xiii. 54-58.
  Mark vi. 1-6.
(He is despised and rejected.)
Galilee.
His Third Journey.
  Matt. ix. 35-38.
  Matt. x. 1-42.
  Matt. xi. 1-
  Mark vi. 6-13.
  Luke ix. 1-6.
He sends the twelve forth to preach.

A prophet is not without honor, save in his own country and among his own kin, and in his own house.

The harvest truly is plenteous but the laborers are few. Pray ye therefore the Lord of the harvest, that he send forth laborers into his harvest.

Go not into *any* way of the Gentiles, and enter not into any

HIS WORDS.

city of the Samaritans: but go rather to the lost sheep of the house of Israel. And as ye go, preach, saying, The kingdom of heaven is at hand. Heal the sick, raise the dead, cleanse the lepers, cast out devils: freely ye received, freely give. Get you no gold, nor silver, nor brass in your purses: no wallet for your journey, neither two coats, nor staff, but go shod with sandals: for the laborer is worthy of his food. And into whatsoever city or village ye shall enter, search out who in it is worthy; and there abide till ye go forth. And as ye enter into the house, salute it. And if the house be worthy, let your peace come upon it: but if it be not worthy, let your peace return to you. And whosoever shall not receive you, nor hear your words, as ye go forth out of that house or that city, shake off the dust of your feet. Verily I say unto you, It shall be more tolerable for the land of Sodom and Gomorrah in the day of judgement, than for that city.

Behold, I send you forth as sheep in the midst of wolves: be ye therefore wise as serpents and harmless as doves. But beware of men: for they will deliver you up to councils, and in their synagogues they will scourge you; yea, and before governors and kings shall ye be brought for my sake, for a testimony to them and to the Gentiles. But when they deliver you up, be not anxious how or what ye shall speak: for it shall be given you in that hour what ye shall speak. For it is not ye that speak, but the Spirit of your Father that speaketh in you. And brother shall deliver up brother to death, and the father his child: and children shall rise up against parents, and cause them to be put to death. And ye shall be hated of all men for my name's sake: but he that endureth to the end, the same shall be saved. But when they persecute you in this city, flee into the next; for verily I say unto you, Ye shall not have gone through the cities of Israel, till the Son of man be come.

A disciple is not above his master, nor a servant above his lord. It is enough for the disciple that he be as his master, and the servant as his lord. If they have called the master of the house Beelzebub, how much more *shall they call* them of his household! Fear them not therefore: for there is nothing covered that shall not be revealed; and hid, that shall not be known. What I tell you in the darkness, speak ye in the light: and what ye hear in the ear, proclaim upon the housetops. And be not afraid of them which kill the body, but are not able to

HIS WORDS.

kill the soul: but rather fear him which is able to destroy both soul and body in hell. Are not two sparrows sold for a farthing? and not one of them shall fall on the ground without your Father: but the very hairs of your head are all numbered. Fear not therefore; ye are of more value than many sparrows. Every one therefore who shall confess me before men, him will I also confess before my Father which is in heaven. But whosoever shall deny me before men, him will I also deny before my Father which is in heaven. Think not that I came to send peace on the earth: I came not to send peace, but a sword. For I came to set a man at variance against his father, and the daughter against her mother, and the daughter-in-law against her mother-in-law: and a man's foes *shall be* they of his own household. He that loveth father or mother more than me is not worthy of me. And he that loveth son or daughter more than me is not worthy of me. And he that doth not take his cross and follow after me, is not worthy of me. He that findeth his life shall lose it; and he that loseth his life for my sake shall find it.

He that receiveth you receiveth me, and he that receiveth me receiveth him that sent me. He that receiveth a prophet in the name of a prophet shall receive a prophet's reward; and he that receiveth a righteous man in the name of a righteous man shall receive a righteous man's reward. And whosoever shall give to drink unto one of these little ones a cup of cold water only, in the name of a disciple, verily I say unto you, he shall in no wise lose his reward.

HIS ACTS.

J. C.
33.
April.

Matt. xiv.1-21.
Mark vi. 14-44.
Luke ix. 7-17.
John vi. 7-14.

John beheaded by Herod.

Jesus and Disciples cross the Sea of Galilee.

He heals many sick, blesses the five loaves and two fishes, and feeds the multitude, over 5000 persons, near Bethsaida.

Come ye yourselves apart unto a desert place, and rest awhile to eat.

Philip, whence are we to buy bread, that these may eat? they have no need to go away: How many loaves have ye? go

HIS ACTS.	HIS WORDS.
	and see,—Bring them hither to me, make the people sit down by companies upon the grass, about fifty each:—give ye them to eat. Gather up the broken pieces which remain over, that nothing be lost.
He goes on the mountain to pray. Walks upon the Sea of Galilee, in the night, and heals many at Gennesaret. Matt. xiv. 22–36. Mark vi. 45–52.	Be of good cheer; It is I, be not afraid. (To Peter,) Come. (Sinking.) O thou of little faith wherefore didst thou doubt?
(The people would make him King, and He withdraws to the Mountain.) Capernaum. Synagogue. John vi. 15–71. His discourse offends, and many turn back. Peter Asserts His Faith.	Verily, verily, I say unto you, Ye seek me, not because ye saw signs, but because ye ate of the loaves, and were filled. Work not for the meat which perisheth, but for the meat which abideth unto eternal life, which the Son of man shall give unto you: for

him the Father, *even* God, hath sealed. . . .

This is the work of God, that ye believe on him whom he hath sent. . . . . .

Verily, verily, I say unto you, It was not Moses that gave you the bread out of heaven; but my Father giveth you the true bread out of heaven. For the bread of God is that which cometh down out of heaven, and giveth life unto the world. . .

I am the bread of life: he that cometh to me shall not hunger, and he that believeth on me shall never thirst. But I said unto you, that ye have seen me and yet believe not. All that which the Father giveth me shall come unto me; and him that cometh to me I will in no wise cast out. For I am come down from heaven, not to do mine own will, but the will of him that sent me. And this is the will of him that sent me, that of all that which he hath given me I should lose nothing, but should raise it up at the last day. For this is the will of my Father, that every one that beholdeth the Son, and believeth on him, should have eternal life; and I will raise him up at the last day. . .

. . . Murmur not among yourselves. No man can come to me, except the Father which sent me draw him: and I will raise

HIS WORDS.

him up in the last day. It is written in the prophets, And they shall all be taught of God. Every one that hath heard from the Father, and hath learned, cometh unto me. Not that any man hath seen the Father, save he which is from God, he hath seen the Father. Verily, verily, I say unto you, He that believeth hath eternal life. I am the bread of life. Your fathers did eat the manna in the wilderness, and they died. This is the bread which cometh down out of heaven, that a man may eat thereof, and not die. I am the living bread which came down out of heaven: if any man eat of this bread, he shall live forever: yea, and the bread which I will give is my flesh, for the life of the world. . . .

Verily, verily, I say unto you, Except ye eat the flesh of the Son of man, and drink his blood, ye have not life in yourselves. He that eateth my flesh and drinketh my blood hath eternal life; and I will raise him up at the last day. For my flesh is meat indeed, and my blood is drink indeed. He that eateth my flesh and drinketh my blood abideth in me, and I in him. As the living Father sent me, and I live because of the Father, so he that eateth me, he also shall live because of me. This is the bread which came down out of heaven: not as the fathers did eat, and died: he that eateth this bread shall live for ever. .

Doth this cause you to stumble? *What* then if ye should behold the Son of man ascending where he was before? It is the spirit that quickeneth; the flesh profiteth nothing: the words that I have spoken unto you are spirit, and are life. But there are some of you that believe not. . . . . For this cause have I said unto you, that no man can come unto me, except it be given unto him of the Father.

Would ye also go away? Did not I choose you the twelve, and one of you is a devil?

HIS ACTS.

J. C, Matt. xv.1-20.
　　　Mark vii. 1-23.
33. Capernaum.
　　　Commandments of God
Summer.　vs Traditions of men.

Why do ye also transgress the commandment of God because of the tradition of men? For God said, Honor thy father and thy mother: and, He that speaketh evil of father or mother, let him die the death. But ye say, Whosoever shall say to his

HIS WORDS.

father or his mother, That wherewith thou mightest have been profited by me is given *to God;* he shall not honor his father. Ye no longer suffer him to do aught for his father or his mother. And many such like things do ye, making void the word of God because of your tradition. Ye hypocrites, well did Isaiah prophesy of you, saying,

This people honoreth me with their lips;
But their heart is far from me.
But in vain do they worship me.
Teaching *as their* doctrines the precepts of men.

Hear, and understand. Not that which entereth into the mouth defileth the man; but that which proceedeth out of the mouth, this defileth the man. . . . Every plant which my heavenly Father planted not, shall be rooted up. Let them alone: they are blind guides. And if the blind guide the blind, both shall fall into a pit. . . . .
(*To Disciples.*)

Are ye also even yet without understanding? Perceive ye not, that whatsoever goeth into the mouth, goeth not into the heart, but passeth into the belly, and is cast out into the draught? But the things which proceed out of the mouth come forth out of the heart; and they defile the man. For out of the heart come forth evil thoughts, murders, adulteries, fornications, thefts, false witness, railings, coveting, wickedness, deceit, lasciviousness an evil eye, foolishness, these are the things which defile the man: but to eat with unwashen hands defileth not the man.

HIS ACTS.

Region Tyre and Sidon.
Matt. xv. 21-28.
Mark. vii. 24-30.
Heals Daughter of Syrophenician woman.

I was not sent but unto the lost sheep of the house of Israel. (*To the Woman.*) Let the children first be filled: for it is not meet to take the children's bread and cast it to the dogs. . (She claims the dogs' portion.)

O Woman, great is thy faith: for this saying go thy way; be it done unto thee even as thou wilt. The devil is gone out of thy daughter.

Heals the Deaf and Dumb, Lame and Blind.
Mark vii. 31-37.

(Deaf and dumb.) Ephphatha, (be opened) tell no man. .

HIS ACTS.	HIS WORDS.

Decapolis.
  Matt. xv. 29-39.
  Mark viii. 1-9.
Four Thousand Fed.
Seven loaves and fishes.
Seven baskets of fragments left.
	I have compassion on the multitude, because they continue with me now three days, and have nothing to eat: and I would not send them away fasting, lest haply they faint by the way. How many loaves have ye? (Let) the multitude sit down on the ground. (They were al filled.)

Near Magdala.
  Matt. xvi. 1-4.
  Mark viii. 10-12.
Pharisees Seek a Sign.
	(Sighing deeply.) Why doth this generation seek a sign? When it is evening, ye say,

It will be fair weather: for the heaven is red. And in the morning, *It will be* foul weather to-day: for the heaven is red and lowring. Ye know how to discern the face of the heaven; but ye cannot *discern* the signs of the times. An evil and adulterous generation seeketh after a sign; and there shall no sign be given unto it, but the sign of Jonah.

Galilee.
  Matt. xvi. 5-12.
  Mark viii. 13-21.
Beware of the leaven of the Pharisees.
	Take heed and beware of the leaven of the Pharisees and Sadduces, and the leaven of Herod. . . . . O ye of little faith, why reason ye among yourselves

because ye have no bread? Do ye not yet perceive, neither understand? Have ye your heart hardened? having eyes, see ye not? and having ears, hear ye not? neither remember the five loaves of the five thousand, and how many baskets ye took up? neither the seven loaves of the four thousand, and how many baskets ye took up? How is it that ye do not perceive that I spake not to you concerning bread? But beware of the leaven of the Pharisees and Sadduces.

Bethsaida.
Heals Blind Man.
  Mark viii. 22-26.
Cesarea Philippi,
  Matt. xvi. 13-28.
  Mark viii. 27-39.
  Luke ix. 18-27.
Disciples profess their faith. Death and resurrection foretold.
	Seest thou aught? Do not even enter into the village. Who do men say that the Son of man is? . . But who do ye say that I am? Peter answered, Thou art the Son of the living God. Blessed art thou, Simon Bar

HIS WORDS.

Jonah: for flesh and blood hath not revealed it unto thee, but my Father which is in heaven. And I also say unto thee, that thou art Peter, and upon this rock I will build my church; and the gates of Hades shall not prevail against it. I will give unto thee the keys of the kingdom of heaven: and whatsoever thou shalt bind on earth shall be bound in heaven: and whatsoever thou shalt loose on earth shall be loosed in heaven. Then charged he the disciples that they should tell no man that he was the Christ. And told them that he must go unto Jerusalem, and suffer many things, and be rejected by the elders and chief priests and scribes, and be killed, and the third day be raised up. . . . .
(Rebukes Peter.) Get thee behind me, Satan: thou art a stumblingblock unto me: for thou mindest not the things of God, but the things of men. . . . . .

If any man would come after me, let him deny himself, and take up his cross, and follow me. For whosoever would save his life shall lose it: and whosoever shall lose his life for my sake and the Gospel's shall find it. For what shall a man be profited, if he shall gain the whole world, and forfeit his life? or what shall a man give in exchange for his life?

For whosoever shall be ashamed of me and of my words in this adulterous and sinful generation, the Son of man also shall be ashamed of him. . . .

For the Son of man shall come in the glory of his Father, with his angels; and then shall he render unto every man according to his deeds. Verily I say unto you, There be some of them that stand here, which shall in no wise taste of death, till they see the kingdom of God come with power.

HIS ACTS.

Cesarea Philippi.
Transfiguration.
Mt. Hermon (or Tabor.)
Matt. xvii. 1-13.
Mark ix. 2-13.

(He talks with Moses and Elijah.)
(*To Disciples*)
Arise, and be not afraid.
Tell the vision to no man, until the Son of man be risen from the dead. Elijah indeed cometh, and shall restore all things: but I say unto you, that Elijah is come already, and they

HIS ACTS.

Heals Demoniac Boy.
　Matt. xvii. 14-21.
　Mark ix. 14-29.
　Luke ix. 37-43.

Disciples Failed.

Galilee.
　Matt. xvii. 22-23.
　Mark ix. 30-32.
　Luke ix. 44-45.
Speaks again of his resurrection.

Capernaum.
Tribute money miraculously provided.
　Matt. xvii. 24-27.

HIS WORDS.

knew him not, but did unto him whatsoever they listed. Even so shall the Son of man also suffer of them.

What question ye with them? O faithless and perverse generation, how long shall I be with you? how long shall I bear with you? bring him hither to me. How long is it since this hath come unto him? If thou canst: all things are possible to him that believeth.

Thou dumb and deaf spirit, I command thee, Come out of him, and enter no more into him.

(*To His Disciples.*)

Because of your little faith: for verily I say unto you, If ye have faith as a grain of mustard seed, ye shall say unto this mountain, Remove hence to yonder place and it shall remove: and nothing, shall be impossible unto you: this kind can come out by nothing, save by prayer.

Let these words sink into your ears: for the Son of man shall be delivered up into the hands of men: and they shall kill him; and when he is killed, after three days he shall rise again.

What thinkest thou, Simon? the kings of the earth, from whom do they receive toll or tribute? from their sons, or from strangers? . . Therefore the sons are free. But, lest we cause them to stumble, go thou to the sea, and cast a hook, and take up the fish that first cometh

HIS ACTS. | ## HIS WORDS.

| | up; and when thou hast opened his mouth, thou shalt find a shekel: that take, and give unto them for me and thee.
Capernaum.
Who Shall be Greatest?
Matt. xviii. 1-35.
Mark ix. 33-50.
Luke ix. 46-50. | What were ye reasoning in the way? . . . If any man would be first, he shall be last of all and minister of all: for he that is least among you, the same is great.

(Taking a little child in his arms.)

Verily I say unto you, Except ye turn, and become as little children, ye shall in no wise enter into the kingdom of heaven. Whosoever therefore shall humble himself as this little child, the same is the greatest in the kingdom of heaven. And whoso shall receive one such little child in my name receiveth me; and whosoever shall receive me receiveth him that sent me: but whoso shall cause one of these little ones which believe on me to stumble, it is profitable for him that a great millstone should be hanged about his neck, and *that* he should be sunk in the depth of the sea. Woe unto the world because of occasions of stumbling! for it must needs be that the occasions come; but woe to that man through whom the occasion cometh! And if thy hand or thy foot causeth thee to stumble, cut it off, and cast it from thee: it is good for thee to enter into life maimed or halt, rather than having two hands or two feet to be cast into the eternal fire. And if thine eye causeth thee to stumble, pluck it out, and cast it from thee: it is good for thee to enter into life with one eye, rather than having two eyes to be cast into the hell of fire. See that ye despise not one of these little ones; for I say unto you, that in heaven their angels do always behold the face of my Father which is in heaven. How think ye? if any man have a hundred sheep, and one of them be gone astray, doth he not leave the ninety and nine, and go unto the mountains, and seek that which goeth astray? And if so be that he find it, verily I say unto you, he rejoiceth over it more than over the ninety and nine which have not gone astray. Even so it is not the will of your Father which is in heaven, that one of these little ones should perish.

And if thy brother sin against thee, go shew him his fault between thee and him alone: if he hear thee, thou hast gained thy brother. But if he hear *thee* not, take with thee one or two

HIS WORDS.

more, that at the mouth of two witnesses or three every word may be established. And if he refuse to hear them, tell it unto the church: and if he refuse to hear the church also, let him be unto thee as the Gentile and the publican. Verily I say unto you, What things soever ye shall bind on earth shall be bound in heaven: and what things soever ye shall loose on earth shall be loosed in heaven. Again I say unto you, that if two of you shall agree on earth as touching any thing that they shall ask, it shall be done for them of my Father which is in heaven. For where two or three are gathered together in my name, there am I in the midst of them.

Forgiveness of Injuries. | Peter said, Lord, how oft shall my brother sin against me, and I forgive him? . . I say not unto thee, Until seven; but, Until seventy times seven. Therefore is the kingdom of heaven likened unto a certain king, which would make a reckoning with his servants. And when he had begun to reckon, one was brought unto him, which owed him ten thousand talents. But forasmuch as he had not *wherewith* to pay, his lord commanded him to be sold, and his wife, and children, and all that he had, and payment to be made. The servant therefore fell down and worshipped him, saying, Lord, have patience with me, and I will pay thee all. And the lord of that servant, being moved with compassion, released him, and forgave him the debt. But that servant went out, and found one of his fellow-servants, which owed him a hundred pence: and he laid hold on him, and took *him* by the throat, saying, Pay what thou owest. So his fellow-servant fell down and besought him, saying, Have patience with me, and I will pay thee. And he would not: but went and cast him into prison, till he should pay that which was due. So when his fellow-servants saw what was done, they were exceeding sorry, and came and told unto their lord all that was done. Then his lord called him unto him, and saith to him, Thou wicked servant, I forgave thee all that debt, because thou besoughtest me: shouldest not thou also have had mercy on thy fellow-servant, even as I had mercy on thee? And his lord was wroth, and delivered him to the tormentors, till he should pay all that was due. So shall also my heavenly Father do unto you, if ye forgive not every one his brother from your hearts.

| HIS ACTS. | HIS WORDS. |

To John who forbade one casting out devils. | (Christian Fellowship.)
. . . Forbid him not: for there is no man which shall do a mighty work in my name, and be able quickly to speak evil of me. For he that is not against us is for us. For whosoever shall give you a cup of water to drink, because ye are Christ's, verily I say unto you, he shall in no wise lose his reward. And whosoever shall cause one of these little ones that believe on me to stumble, it were better for him if a great millstone were hanged about his neck, and he were cast into the sea. And if thy hand cause thee to stumble, cut it off: it is good for thee to enter into life maimed, rather than having thy two hands to go into hell, into the unquenchable fire. And if thy foot cause thee to stumble, cut it off: it is good for thee to enter into life halt, rather than having thy two feet to be cast into hell. And if thine eye cause thee to stumble, cast it out: it is good for thee to enter into the kingdom of God with one eye, rather than having two eyes to be cast into hell; where their worm dieth not, and the fire is not quenched. For every one shall be salted with fire. Salt is good: but if the salt have lost its saltness, wherewith will ye season it? Have salt in yourselves, and be at peace one with another.

John vii. 1-8.
Tarries in Galilee.
His Time not Come. | . . . My time is not yet come; but your time is alway ready. The world cannot hate you; but me it hateth, because I testify of it, that its works are evil. Go ye up unto the feast: I go not up yet unto this feast; because my time is not yet fulfilled. . . . .

Jerusalem.
John vii. 11, to viii 1. | . . . My teaching is not mine, but his that sent me. If any man willeth to do his will, he shall know of the teaching, whether it be of God, or *whether* I speak from myself. He that speaketh from himself seeketh his own glory: but he that seeketh the glory of him that sent him, the same is true, and no unrighteousness is in him. Did not Moses give you the law, and *yet* none of you doeth the law? Why seek ye to kill me? . . . .

I did one work, and ye all marvel. For this cause hath Moses given you circumcision (not that it is of Moses, but of the fathers); and on the Sabbath ye circumcise a man. If a man receiveth circumcision on the Sabbath, that the law of Moses

HIS WORDS.

may not be broken, are ye wroth with me, because I made a man every whit whole on the Sabbath? Judge not according to appearance, but judge righteous judgment.

. . Ye both know me, and know whence I am; and I am not come of myself, but he that sent me is true, whom ye know not. I know him; because I am from him, and he sent me.

. . . Yet a little while am I with you, and I go unto him that sent me. Ye shall seek me, and shall not find me: and where I am, ye cannot come. . . . .

. . . If any man thirst, let him come unto me, and drink. He that believeth on me, as the Scripture hath said, out of his belly shall flow rivers of living water. . . . .

HIS ACTS.

Enroute to Jerusalem. Samaritans inhospitable. Disciples rebuked for anger.
Luke ix. 51-56.
Returns from Mount of Olives.
Woman taken in adultery.
John viii. 2-11.

Errata.—This incident should have appeared on page thirty-six, previous to arrival at Jerusalem.

. . . Ye know not what manner of spirit ye are of.

(*To Her Accusers.*)
He that is without sin among you, let him first cast a stone at her. . . .

Woman, where are they? did no man condemn thee? . . Neither do I condemn thee: go thy way: from henceforth sin no more.

Discourse in Temple.
John viii. 12.

. . I am the light of the world: he that followeth me shall not walk in the darkness, but shall have the light of life.
. . . (The Pharisees, Thou bearest witness of thyself; thy witness is not true.) (Jesus answered), Even if I bear witness of myself, my witness is true; for I know whence I came, and whither I go; but ye know not whence I come, or whither I go. Ye judge after the flesh: I judge no man. Yea, and if I judge, my judgment is true; for I am not alone, but I and the Father that sent me. Yea, and in your law it is written, that the witness of two men is true. I am he that beareth witness of myself, and the Father that sent me beareth witness of me. . . Ye know neither me, nor my Father: if ye knew me, ye would know my Father also. .

HIS WORDS.

. . . I go away, and ye shall seek me, and shall die in your sin: whither I go, ye cannot come. . . . Ye are from beneath; I am from above: ye are of this world; I am not of this world. I said therefore unto you, that ye shall die in your sins: for except ye believe that I am *he*, ye shall die in your sins. . . . . .

Even that which I have also spoken unto you from the beginning. I have many things to speak and to judge concerning you: howbeit he that sent me is true; and the things which I heard from him, these speak I unto the world. . . . When ye have lifted up the Son of man, then shall ye know that I am *he*, and *that* I do nothing of myself, but as the Father taught me, I speak these things. And he that sent me is with me; he hath not left me alone; for I do always the things that are pleasing to him. . . . . .

. . . If ye abide in my word, *then* are ye truly my disciples; and ye shall know the truth, and the truth shall make you free. . . . .

Verily, verily, I say unto you, Every one that committeth sin is the bond-servant of sin. And the bond-servant abideth not in the house for ever: the Son abideth for ever. If therefore the Son shall make you free, ye shall be free indeed. I know that ye are Abraham's seed; yet ye seek to kill me, because my word hath not free course in you. . I speak the things which I have seen with *my* Father: and ye also do the things which ye heard from *your* father. . . . .

If ye were Abraham's children, ye would do the works of Abraham. But now ye seek to kill me, a man that hath told you the truth, which I heard from God: this did not Abraham. Ye do the works of your father. If God were your Father, ye would love me: for I came forth and am come from God; for neither have I come of myself, but he sent me. Why do ye not understand my speech? *Even* because ye cannot hear my word. Ye are of *your* father the devil, and the lusts of your father it is your will to do. He was a murderer from the beginning, and stood not in the truth, because there is no truth in him. When he speaketh a lie, he speaketh of his own: for he is a liar, and the father thereof. But because I say the truth, ye believe me not. Which of you convicteth me of sin? If I say truth, why do ye not believe me? He that is of God heareth the words of God: for this cause ye hear *them* not, because ye are not of God. .

HIS WORDS.

I have not a devil: but I honor my Father, and ye dishonor me. But I seek not mine own glory: there is one that seeketh and judgeth. Verily, verily, I say unto you, If a man keep my word, he shall never see death. . . . .

If I glorify myself, my glory is nothing: it is my Father that glorifieth me; of whom ye say, that he is your God; and ye have not known him: but I know him; and if I should say, I know him not, I shall be like unto you, a liar: but I know him, and keep his word. Your father Abraham rejoiced to see my day; and he saw it, and was glad. . . . Verily, verily, I say unto you, Before Abraham was, I am. . . .
(*To Disciples.*)

HIS ACTS.

Jerusalem.
John ix. 1--41.
Heals blind man on Sabbath.

. . . Neither did this man sin, nor his parents: but that the works of God should be made manifest in him. We must work the works of him that sent me, while it is day: the night cometh, when no man can work. When I am in the world, I am the light of the world. . . . .
(*To Blind Man.*)
Go, wash in the pool of Siloam.
. . . Dost thou believe on the Son of God? . . Thou hast both seen him, and he it is that speaketh with thee. . . For judgment came I into this world, that they which see not may see; and that they which see may become blind.
(*To the Pharisees.*)
. . . If ye were blind, ye would have no sin: but now ye say, We see: your sin remaineth.

John x. 1--18.
The Good Shepherd.

Verily, verily, I say unto you, He that entereth not by the door into the fold of the sheep, but climbeth up some other way, the same is a thief and a robber. But he that entereth in by the door is the shepherd of the sheep. To him the porter openeth; and the sheep hear his voice: and he calleth his own sheep by name, and leadeth them out. When he hath put forth all his own, he goeth before them, and the sheep follow him: for they know his voice. And a stranger will they not follow, but will flee from him: for they know not the voice of strangers. Verily, verily, I say unto you, I am the door of the sheep. All that came before me are

HIS WORDS.

thieves and robbers: but the sheep did not hear them. I am the door: by me if any man enter in, he shall be saved, and shall go in and go out, and shall find pasture. The thief cometh not, but that he may steal, and kill, and destroy: I came that they may have life, and may have *it* abundantly. I am the good shepherd: the good shepherd layeth down his life for the sheep. He that is a hireling, and not a shepherd, whose own the sheep are not, beholdeth the wolf coming, and leaveth the sheep, and fleeth, and the wolf snatcheth them, and scattereth *them: he fleeth* because he is a hireling, and careth not for the sheep. I am the good shepherd; and I know mine own, and mine own know me, even as the Father knoweth me, and I know the Father; and I lay down my life for the sheep. And other sheep I have, which are not of this fold: them also I must bring, and they shall hear my voice; and they shall become one flock, one shepherd. Therefore doth the Father love me, because I lay down my life, that I may take it again. No one taketh it away from me, but I lay it down of myself. I have power to lay it down, and I have power to take it again. This commandment received I from my Father.

HIS ACTS.

Seventy Disciples sent forth at Capernaum, and return.
Luke x. 1--24.

. . . The harvest is plenteous, but the laborers are few: pray ye therefore the Lord of the harvest, that he send forth laborers into his harvest. Go your ways: behold, I send you forth as lambs in the midst of wolves. Carry no purse, no wallet, no shoes: and salute no man on the way. And into whatsoever house ye shall enter, first say, Peace *be* to this house. And if a son of peace be there, your peace shall rest upon him: but if not it shall turn to you again. And in that same house remain, eating and drinking such things as they give: for the laborer is worthy of his hire. Go not from house to house. And into whatsoever city ye enter, and they receive you, eat such things as are set before you: and heal the sick that are therein, and say unto them, The kingdom of God is come nigh unto you. But into whatsoever city ye shall enter, and they receive you not, go out into the streets thereof and say, Even the dust from your city, that cleaveth to our feet, we do wipe off against you: howbeit know this, that the kingdom of God is come nigh. I say unto you, It shall be more tolerable in that day for Sodom, than for

HIS WORDS.

that city. Woe unto thee, Chorazin! woe unto thee, Bethsaida! for if the mighty works had been done in Tyre and Sidon, which were done in you, they would have repented long ago, sitting in sackcloth and ashes. Howbeit it shall be more tolerable for Tyre and Sidon in the judgment, than for you. And thou, Capernaum, shalt thou be exalted unto heaven? thou shalt be brought down unto Hades. He that heareth you heareth me; and he that rejecteth you rejecteth me; and he that rejecteth me rejecteth him that sent me.

. . . I beheld Satan fallen as lightning from heaven. Behold, I have given you authority to tread upon serpents and scorpions, and over all the power of the enemy: and nothing shall in any wise hurt you. Howbeit in this rejoice not, that the spirits are subject unto you; but rejoice that your names are written in heaven.

In that same hour he rejoiced in the Holy Spirit, and said, I thank thee, O Father, Lord of heaven and earth, that thou didst hide these things from the wise and understanding, and didst reveal them unto babes: yea, Father; for so it was well-pleasing in thy sight. All things have been delivered unto me of my Father: and no one knoweth who the Son is, save the Father; and who the Father is, save the Son, and he to whomsoever the Son willeth to reveal *him*. . . . .
(*To the Disciples.*)

. . . Blessed *are* the eyes which see the things that ye see: for I say unto you, that many prophets and kings desired to see the things which ye see, and saw them not: and to hear the things which ye hear, and heard them not.

HIS ACTS.

A lawyer questions him of eternal life, etc.
Luke x. 25--37.

Who is my neighbor?
The Good Samaritan.

. . . What is written in the law? how readest thou? . . . . Thou hast answered right: this do, and thou shalt live.

. . . A certain man was going down from Jerusalem to Jericho; and he fell among robbers, which both stripped him and beat him, and departed, leaving him half dead. And by chance a certain priest was going down that way: and when he saw him, he passed by on the other side. And in like manner a Levite also, when he came to the place, and saw him, passed by

HIS WORDS.

on the other side. But a certain Samaritan, as he journeyed, came where he was: and when he saw him, he was moved with compassion, and came to him, and bound up his wounds, pouring on *them* oil and wine; and he set him on his own beast, and brought him to an inn, and took care of him. And on the morrow he took out two pence, and gave them to the host, and said, Take care of him; and whatsoever thou spendest more, I, when I come back again, will repay thee. Which of these three, thinkest thou, proved neighbor unto him that fell among the robbers? . . . . Go, and do thou likewise.

HIS ACTS.

Bethany.
Mary and Martha.
   Luke xi. 38--42.
Near Jerusalem.
   Luke xi. 1--13.
Disciples taught to pray.

. . . Martha, Martha, thou art anxious and troubled about many things: but one thing is needful: for Mary hath chosen the good part, which shall not be taken away from her.

When ye pray, say, Father Hallowed be thy name. Thy kingdom come. Give us day by day our daily bread. And forgive us our sins; for we ourselves also forgive every one that is indebted to us. And bring us not into temptation.

. . . Which of you shall have a friend, and shall go unto him at midnight, and say to him, Friend, lend me three loaves; for a friend of mine is come to me from a journey, and I have nothing to set before him; and he from within shall answer and say, Trouble me not: the door is now shut, and my children are with me in bed: I cannot rise and give thee? I say unto you, Though he will not rise and give him, because he is his friend, yet because of his importunity he will arise and give him as many as he needeth. And I say unto you, Ask, and it shall be given you; seek, and ye shall find; knock, and it shall be opened unto you. For every one that asketh receiveth; and he that seeketh findeth; and to him that knocketh it shall be opened. And of which of you that is a father shall his son ask a loaf, and he give him a stone? Or a fish, and he for a fish give him a serpent? Or *if* he shall ask an egg, will he give him a scorpion? If ye then, being evil, know how to give good gifts unto your children, how much more shall *your* heavenly Father give the Holy Spirit to them that ask him?

HIS ACTS.	HIS WORDS.
Galilee. Luke xi. 37--54. Luke xii. 1--59. Luke xiii. 1--9. Pharisee's Table. Denounces them.	Now do ye Pharisees cleanse the outside of the cup and of the platter; but your inward part is full of extortion and wickedness. Ye foolish ones, did not he that made the outside make the in-

side also? Howbeit give for alms those things which are within; and behold, all things are clean unto you.

But woe unto you, Pharisees! for ye tithe mint and rue and every herb, and pass over judgment and the love of God: but these ought ye to have done, and not to leave the other undone. Woe unto you, Pharisees! for ye love the chief seats in the synagogues, and the salutations in the marketplaces. Woe unto you! for ye are as the tombs which appear not, and the men that walk over *them* know it not.

. . Woe unto you lawyers also! for ye lade men with burdens grievous to be borne, and ye yourselves touch not the burdens with one of your fingers. Woe unto you! for ye build the tombs of the prophets, and your fathers killed them. So ye are witnesses and consent unto the works of your fathers: for they killed them, and ye build *their tombs*. Therefore also said the wisdom of God, I will send unto them prophets and apostles, and *some* of them they shall kill and persecute; that the blood of all the prophets, which was shed from the foundation of the world, may be required of this generation; from the blood of Abel unto the blood of Zachariah, who perished between the altar and the sanctuary. Yea, I say unto you, It shall be required of this generation. Woe unto you lawyers! for ye took away the key of knowledge: ye entered not in yourselves, and them that were entering in ye hindered.

. . Beware ye of the leaven of the Pharisees, which is hypocrisy. But there is nothing covered up that shall not be revealed: and hid, that shall not be known. Wherefore whatsoever ye have said in the darkness shall be heard in the light; and what ye have spoken in the ear in the inner chambers shall be proclaimed upon the housetops. And I say unto you, my friends, be not afraid of them which kill the body, and after that they have no more that they can do. But I will warn you whom ye shall fear. Fear him, which after he hath killed hath power to cast into hell; yea, I say unto you, Fear him. Are not five sparrows sold for two farthings? and not one of them is forgotten in the

HIS WORDS.

sight of God. But the very hairs of your head are all numbered. Fear not: ye are of more value than many sparrows. And I say unto you, Every one who shall confess me before men, him shall the Son of man also confess before the angels of God: but he that denieth me in the presence of men shall be denied in the presence of the angels of God. And every one who shall speak a word against the Son of man, it shall be forgiven him: but unto him that blasphemeth against the Holy Spirit it shall not be forgiven. And when they bring you before the synagogues, and the rulers, and the authorities, be not anxious how or what ye shall answer, or what ye shall say: for the Holy Spirit shall teach you in that very hour what ye ought to say.

(To one who asked him to arbitrate an estate.) . . . . . Man, who made me a judge or a divider over you? . . Take heed, and keep yourselves from all covetousness: for a man's life consisteth not in the abundance of the things which he possesseth.

. . The ground of a certain rich man brought forth plentifully: and he reasoned within himself, saying, What shall I do, because I have not where to bestow my fruits? And he said, This will I do: I will pull down my barns, and build greater; and there will I bestow all my corn and my goods. And I will say to my soul, Soul, thou hast much goods laid up for many years; take thine ease, eat, drink, be merry. But God said unto him, Thou foolish one, this night is thy soul required of thee; and the things which thou hast prepared, whose shall they be? So is he that layeth up treasure for himself, and is not rich toward God.

. . Be not anxious for your life, what ye shall eat; nor yet for your body, what ye shall put on. For the life is more than the food, and the body than the raiment. Consider the ravens, that they sow not, neither reap; which have no store-chamber nor barn; and God feedeth them: of how much more value are ye than the birds! And which of you by being anxious can add a cubit unto his stature? If then ye are not able to do even that which is least, why are ye anxious concerning the rest? Consider the lilies, how they grow: they toil not, neither do they spin: yet I say unto you, Even Solomon in all his glory was not arrayed like one of these. But if God doth so clothe the grass in the field, which to-day is, and to-morrow is cast into the oven; how much more shall he clothe you, O ye of

HIS WORDS.

little faith? And seek not ye what ye shall eat, and what ye shall drink, neither be ye of doubtful mind. For all these things do the nations of the world seek after: but your Father knoweth that ye have need of these things. Howbeit seek ye his kingdom: and these things shall be added unto you. Fear not, little flock; for it is your Father's good pleasure to give you the kingdom. Sell that ye have, and give alms; make for yourselves purses which wax not old, a treasure in the heavens that faileth not, where no thief draweth near, neither moth destroyeth. For where your treasure is, there will your heart be also.

Let your loins be girded about, and your lamps burning; and be ye yourselves like unto men looking for their lord, when he shall return from the marriage feast; that when he cometh and knocketh, they may straightway open unto him. Blessed are those servants, whom the lord when he cometh shall find watching; verily I say unto you, that he shall gird himself, and make them sit down to meat, and shall come and serve them. And if he shall come in the second watch, and if in the third, and find them so, blessed are those servants. But know this, that if the master of the house had known in what hour the thief was coming, he would have watched, and not have left his house to be broken through. Be ye also ready: for in an hour that ye think not the Son of man cometh.

. . Who then is the faithful and wise steward, whom his lord shall set over his household, to give them their portion of food in due season? Blessed is that servant, whom his lord when he cometh shall find so doing. Of a truth I say unto you, that he will set him over all that he hath. But if that servant shall say in his heart, My lord delayeth his coming; and shall begin to beat the men-servants and the maid-servants, and to eat and drink, and to be drunken; the lord of that servant shall come in a day when he expecteth not, and in an hour when he knoweth not, and shall cut him asunder, and appoint his portion with the unfaithful. And that servant, which knew his lord's will, and made not ready, nor did according to his will, shall be beaten with many stripes; but he that knew not, and did things worthy of stripes, shall be beaten with few stripes. And to whomsoever much is given, of him shall much be required: and to whom they commit much, of him will they ask the more.

I came to cast fire upon the earth; and what will I, if it is already kindled? But I have a baptism to be baptized with;

HIS WORDS.

and how am I straitened till it be accomplished! Think ye that I am come to give peace in the earth? I tell you, Nay: but rather division: for there shall be from henceforth five in one house divided, three against two, and two against three. They shall be divided, father against son, and son against father; mother against daughter, and daughter against her mother; mother-in-law against her daughter-in-law, and daughter-in-law against her mother-in-law.

. . When ye see a cloud rising in the west, straightway ye say, There cometh a shower; and so it cometh to pass. And when ye see a south wind blowing, ye say, There will be a scorching heat; and it cometh to pass. Ye hypocrites, ye know how to interpret the face of the earth and the heavens; but how is it that ye know not how to interpret this time? And why even of yourselves judge ye not what is right? For as thou art going with thine adversary before the magistrate, on the way give diligence to be quit of him; lest haply he hale thee unto the judge, and the judge shall deliver thee to the officer, and the officer shall cast thee into prison. I say unto thee, Thou shalt by no means come out thence, till thou have paid the very last mite.

. . Think ye that these Galilæans were sinners above all the Galilæans, because they have suffered these things? I tell you, Nay: but, except ye repent, ye shall all in like manner perish. Or those eighteen, upon whom the tower of Siloam fell, and killed them, think ye that they were offenders above all the men that dwell in Jerusalem? I tell you, Nay, but except ye repent, ye shall all likewise perish.

. . A certain man had a fig-tree planted in his vineyard; and he came seeking fruit thereon, and found none. And he said unto the vinedresser, Behold these three years I come seeking fruit on this fig-tree, and find none: cut it down; why doth it also cumber the ground? And he answering saith unto him, Lord, let it alone this year also, till I shall dig about it, and dung it: and if it bear fruit thenceforth, well, but if not, thou shalt cut it down.

HIS ACTS.

Jerusalem.
John x. 22--39.
Feast of Dedication.
Art thou the Christ?

. . . I told you, and ye believe not: the works that I do in my Father's name, these bear witness of me. But ye believe

HIS WORDS.

not, because ye are not of my sheep. My sheep hear my voice, and I know them, and they follow me: and I give unto them eternal life; and they shall never perish, and no one shall snatch them out of my hand. My Father, which hath given *them* unto me, is greater than all; and no one is able to snatch *them* out of the Father's hand. I and the Father are one. . Many good works have I shewed you from the Father; for which of those works do ye stone me? . . . Is it not written, in your law, I said, Ye are gods? If he called them gods, unto whom the word of God came (and the Scripture cannot be broken), say ye of him, whom the Father sanctified and sent into the world, Thou blasphemest; because I said, I am *the* Son of God? If I do not the works of my Father, believe me not. But if I do them, though ye believe not me, believe the works: that ye may know and understand that the Father is in me, and I in the Father. . . . . .

HIS ACTS.

Bethany.
John xi. 1.–44.
Raising of Lazarus.

. . . This sickness is not unto death, but for the glory of God, that the Son of God may be glorified thereby. . . .

. . . Let us go into Judea again. . . . .
. . . Are there not twelve hours in the day? If a man walk in the day, he stumbleth not, because he seeth the light of this world. But if a man walketh in the night, he stumbleth, because the light is not in him. . . Our friend Lazarus is fallen asleep; but I go, that I may awake him out of sleep. . . Lazarus is dead. And I am glad for your sakes that I was not there, to the intent ye may believe; nevertheless let us go unto him. . .
(*To Martha.*)
Thy brother shall rise again. . . . I am the resurrection, and the life: he that believeth on me, though he die, yet shall he live: and whosoever liveth and believeth on me shall never die. Believest thou this? . . Where have ye laid him? (He weeps). Take ye away the stone.
. . . Said I not unto thee, that, if thou believedst, thou shouldest see the glory of God? . . . (Jesus lifts up his eyes). Father, I thank thee that thou heardest me. And I knew that thou hearest me always: but because of the multitude which standeth around I said it, that they may believe that thou didst send me. . . . (With a loud voice). Lazarus, come forth. . . . Loose him, and let him go.

HIS ACTS.

J. C. Perea,
Valley of Jordan.
33. Matt. xix. 1–2.
Mark x. 1.
Luke xiii. 10–35.
Heals an infirm woman on the Sabbath.

HIS WORDS.

Woman, thou art loosed from thine infirmity . . Ye hypocrites, doth not each of you on the Sabbath loose his ox or his ass from the stall, and lead him away to watering? And ought not this woman, being a daughter of Abraham, whom Satan had bound, lo, *these* eighteen years, to have been loosed from this bond on the day of the Sabbath?

The Kingdom of God.

. . . Unto what is the kingdom of God like? and whereunto shall I liken it? It is like unto a grain of mustard seed, which a man took, and cast into his own garden; and it grew, and became a tree; and the birds of the heaven lodged in the branches thereof. And again he said, Whereunto shall I liken the kingdom of God? It is like unto leaven, which a woman took and hid in three measures of meal, till it was all leavened.

Are Many Saved?

. . . Strive to enter in by the narrow door: for many, I say unto you, shall seek to enter in, and shall not be able. When once the master of the house is risen up, and hath shut to the door, and ye begin to stand without, and to knock at the door, saying, Lord, open to us; and he shall answer and say to you, I know ye not whence ye are; then shall ye begin to say, We did eat and drink in thy presence, and thou didst teach in our streets; and he shall say, I tell you, I know not whence ye are; depart from me, all ye workers of iniquity. There shall be the weeping and gnashing of teeth, when ye shall see Abraham, and Isaac, and Jacob, and all the prophets, in the kingdom of God, and yourselves cast forth without. And they shall come from the east and west, and from the north and south, and shall sit down in the kingdom of God. And behold, there are last which shall be first, and there are first which shall be last.

Warned Against Herod.

. . . Go and say to that fox, Behold, I cast out devils and perform cures to-day and to-morrow, and the third *day* I am perfected. Howbeit I must go on my way to day and to-morrow and the *day* following: for it cannot be that a prophet perish out of Jerusalem. O Jerusalem, Jerusalem, which killeth the prophets, and stoneth them that are sent unto her! how

HIS WORDS.

often would I have gathered thy children together, even as a hen *gathereth* her own brood under her wings, and ye would not! Behold, your house is left unto you *desolate:* and I say unto you, Ye shall not see me, until ye shall say, Blessed is he that cometh in the name of the Lord.

HIS ACTS.

Perea.
Luke xiv. 1-24.
Eats at Pharisee House.
Heals man of Dropsy on the Sabbath.

. . . Is it lawful to heal on the Sabbath, or not? . . Which of you shall have an ass or an ox fallen into a well, and will not straightway draw him up on a Sabbath day? . .

Humility.

. . . When thou art bidden of any man to a marriage feast, sit not down in the chief seat; lest haply a more honorable man than thou be bidden of him, and he that bade thee and him shall come and say to thee, Give this man place; and then thou shalt begin with shame to take the lowest place But when thou art bidden, go and sit down in the lowest; that when he that hath bidden thee cometh, he may say to thee, Friend, go up higher: then shalt thou have glory in the presence of all that sit at meat with thee. For every one that exalteth himself shall be humbled; and he that humbleth himself shall be exalted.

Duty to the poor, etc.

. . . When thou makest a dinner or a supper, call not thy friends, nor thy brethren, nor thy kinsmen, nor rich neighbors; lest haply they also bid thee again, and a recompense be made thee. But when thou makest a feast, bid the poor, the maimed, the lame, the blind: and thou shalt be blessed; because they have not *wherewith* to recompense thee: for thou shalt be recompensed in the resurrection of the just.

The great supper, who are rejected?

. . . A certain man made a great supper; and he bade many: and he sent forth his servant at supper time to say to them that were bidden, Come; for *all* things are now ready. And they all with one *consent* began to make excuse. The first said unto him, I have bought a field, and I must needs go out and see it: I pray thee have me excused. And another said, I have bought five yoke of oxen, and I go to prove them: I pray thee have me excused. And another said, I have married a wife, and therefore I cannot come. And the servant came, and told his lord these things. Then the master of the house,

HIS WORDS.

being angry, said to his servant, Go out quickly into the streets and lanes of the city, and bring in hither the poor and maimed and blind and lame. And the servant said, Lord, what thou didst command is done, and yet there is room. And the lord said unto the servant, Go out into the highways and hedges, and constrain *them* to come in, that my house may be filled. For I say unto you, that none of these men which were bidden shall taste of my supper.

HIS ACTS.

Cross-bearing.
Luke xiv. 25-35.

. . . If any man cometh unto me, and hateth not his own father and mother, and wife, and children, and brethren, and sisters, yea, and his own life also, he cannot be my disciple. Whosoever doth not bear his own cross, and come after me, cannot be my disciple. For which of you, desiring to build a tower, doth not first sit down and count the cost, whether he have *wherewith* to comp'ete it? Lest haply, when he hath laid a foundation, and is not able to finish, all that behold begin to mock him, saying, This man began to build, and was not able to finish. Or what king, when he goeth to encounter another king in war, will not sit down first and take counsel whether he is able with ten thousand to meet him that cometh against him with twenty thousand? Or else, while the other is yet a great way off, he sendeth an ambassage, and asketh conditions of peace. So therefore whosoever he be of you that renounceth not all that he hath, he cannot be my disciple. Salt therefore is good: but if even the salt have lost its savour, wherewith shall it be seasoned? It is fit neither for the land nor for the dunghill: *men* cast it out. He that ears to hear, let him hear.

The Lost Sheep.

. . . . What man of you, having a hundred sheep, and having lost one of them, doth not leave the ninety and nine in the wilderness, and go after that which is lost, until he find it? And when he hath found it, he layeth it on his shoulders, rejoicing. And when he cometh home, he calleth together his friends and his neighbors, saying unto them, Rejoice with me, for I have found my sheep which was lost. I say unto you, that even so there shall be joy in heaven over one sinner that repenteth, *more* than over ninety and nine righteous persons, which need no repentance.

HIS WORDS.

Or what woman having ten pieces of silver, if she lose one piece, doth not light a lamp, and sweep the house, and seek diligently until she find it? And when she hath found it, she calleth together her friends and neighbors, saying, Rejoice with me, for I have found the piece which I had lost. Even so, I say unto you, there is joy in the presence of the angels of God over one sinner that repenteth.

HIS ACTS.

Prodigal Son.
Luke xv. 1-32.

. . . A certain man had two sons: and the younger of them said to his father, Father, give me the portion of *thy* substance that falleth to me. And he divided unto them his living. And not many days after the younger son gathered all together, and took his journey into a far country; and there he wasted his substance with riotous living. And when he had spent all, there arose a mighty famine in that country; and he began to be in want. And he went and joined himself to one of the citizens of that country; and he sent him into his fields to feed swine. And he would fain have been filled with the husks that the swine did eat: and no man gave unto him. But when he came to himself he said, How many hired servants of my father have bread enough and to spare, and I perish here with hunger! I will arise and go to my father, and will say unto him, Father, I have sinned against heaven, and in thy sight: I am no more worthy to be called thy son: make me as one of thy hired servants. And he arose, and came to his father. But while he was yet afar off, his father saw him, and was moved with compassion, and ran, and fell on his neck, and kissed him. And the son said unto him, Father, I have sinned against heaven and in thy sight: I am no more worthy to be called thy son. But the father said to his servants, Bring forth quickly the best robe, and put it on him; and put a ring on his hand, and shoes on his feet: and bring the fatted calf, *and* kill it, and let us eat, and make merry: for this my son was dead, and is alive again; he was lost, and is found. And they began to be merry. Now his elder son was in the field: and as he came and drew nigh to the house, he heard music and dancing. And he called to him one of the servants, and inquired what these things might be. And he said unto him, Thy brother is come; and thy father hath killed the fatted calf, because he hath received him safe and

HIS WORDS.

sound. But he was angry, and would not go in: and his father came out, and intreated him. But he answered and said to his father, Lo, these many years do I serve thee and I never transgressed a commandment of thine: and *yet* thou never gavest me a kid, that I might make merry with my friends: but when this thy son came, which hath devoured thy living with harlots, thou killedst for him the fatted calf. And he said unto him, Son, thou art ever with me, and all that is mine is thine. But it was meet to make merry and be glad: for this thy brother was dead, and is alive *again;* and *was* lost, and is found.

HIS ACTS.

Perea.
Luke xvi. 1-31.
The Unjust Steward.

There was a certain rich man, which had a steward; and the same was accused unto him that he was wasting his goods. And he called him, and said unto him, What is this that I hear of thee? render the account of thy stewardship; for thou canst be no longer steward. And the steward said within himself, What shall I do, seeing that my lord taketh away the stewardship from me? I have not strength to dig; to beg I am ashamed. I am resolved what to do, that, when I am put out of the stewardship, they may receive me into their houses. And calling to him each one of his lord's debtors, he said to the first, How much owest thou unto my lord? And he said, A hundred measures of oil. And he said unto him, Take thy bond, and sit down quickly and write fifty. Then said he to another, And how much owest thou? And he said, A hundred measures of wheat. He saith unto him, Take thy bond, and write fourscore. And his lord commended the unrighteous steward because he had done wisely: for the sons of this world are for their own generation wiser than the sons of the light. And I say unto you, Make to yourselves friends by means of the mammon of unrighteousness; that, when it shall fail, they may receive you into the eternal tabernacles. He that is faithful in a very little is faithful also in much: and that is unrighteous in a very little is unrighteous also in much. If therefore ye have not been faithful in the unrighteous mammon, who will commit to your trust the true *riches?* And if ye have not been faithful in that which is another's, who will give you that which is your own? No servant can serve two masters: for either he will

HIS WORDS

hate the one, and love the other; or else he will hold to one, and despise the other. Ye cannot serve God and mammon.

HIS ACTS.

Pharisees Reproved. (*To the Pharisees.*) . . . Ye are they that justify yourselves in the sight of men; but God knoweth your hearts: for that which is exalted among men is an abomination in the sight of God. The law and the prophets *were* until John: from that time the gospel of the kingdom of God is preached, and every man entereth violently into it. But it is easier for heaven and earth to pass away, than for one tittle of the law to fall. Every one that putteth away his wife, and marrieth another, committeth adultery: and he that marrieth one that is put away from a husband committeth adultery.

Rich Man and Lazarus. Now there was a certain rich man, and he was clothed in purple and fine linen, faring sumptuously every day: and a certain beggar named Lazarus was laid at his gate, full of sores, and desiring to be fed with the *crumbs* that fell f om the rich man's table; yea, even the dogs came and licked his sores. And it came to pass, that the beggar died, and that he was carried away by the angels into Abraham's bosom: and the rich man also died, and was buried. And in Hades he lifted up his eyes, being in torments, and seeth Abraham afar off, and Lazarus in his bosom. And he cried and said, Father Abraham, have mercy on me, and send Lazarus, that he may dip the tip of his finger in water, and cool my tongue; for I am in anguish in this flame. But Abraham said, Son, remember that thou in thy lifetime receivedst thy good things, and Lazarus in like manner evil things: but now here he is comforted, and thou art in anguish. And beside all this, between us and you there is a great gulf fixed, that they which would pass from hence to you may not be able, and that none may cross over from thence to us. And he said, I pray thee therefore, father, that thou wouldest send him to my father's house; for I have five brethren: that he may testify unto them, lest they also come into this place of torment. But Abraham saith, They have Moses and the prophets: let them hear them. And he said, Nay, father Abraham: but if one go to them from the dead, they will repent. And he said unto him, If they hear not Moses and the prophets, **neither** will they be persuaded, if one rise from the dead.

HIS ACTS.

J. C. Perea.
Luke xvii. 1–37.
33. Forgive Injuries.

Have Faith.

Heals ten lepers.
His Coming Sudden.

HIS WORDS.

It is impossible but that occasions of stumbling should come: but woe unto him through whom they come! It were well for him if a mill stone were hanged about his neck, and he were thrown into the sea, rather than that he should cause one of these little ones to stumble. Take heed to yourselves: if thy brother sin, rebuke him: and if he sin against thee seven times in the day, and seven times turn again to thee, saying, I repent, thou shalt forgive him.

. . . If ye have faith as a grain of mustard seed, ye would say unto this sycamine tree, Be thou rooted up, and be thou planted in the sea; and it would have obeyed you. But who is there of you, having a servant plowing or keeping sheep, that will say unto him, when he come in from the field, Come straightway and sit down to meat; and will not rather say unto him, Make ready wherewith I may sup, and gird thyself, and serve me, till I have eaten and drunken; and afterward thou shalt eat and drink? Doth he thank the servant because he did the things that were commanded? Even so ye also, when ye shall have done all the things that are commanded you, say, We are unprofitable servants; we have done that which it was our duty to do.

. . . Go and shew yourselves unto the priests. Were not the ten cleansed? but where are the nine? Were there none found that returned to give glory to God, save this stranger? . . . Arise, and go thy way: thy faith hath made thee whole. . . The kingdom of God cometh not with observation: neither shall they say, Lo, here! or, There! for lo, the kingdom of God is within you.

. . . The days will come, when ye shall desire to see one of the days of the Son of man, and ye shall not see it. And they shall say to you, Lo, there! Lo, here! go not away, nor follow after them: for as the lightning, when it lighteneth out of the one part under the heaven, shineth unto the other part under heaven; so shall the Son of man be in his day. But first must he suffer many things and be rejected of this generation. And as it came to pass in the days of Noah, even so shall it be also in the days of the Son of man. They ate, they drank,

HIS WORDS.

they married, they were given in marriage, until the day that Noah entered into the ark, and the flood came, and destroyed them all. Likewise even as it came to pass in the days of Lot; they ate, they drank, they bought, they sold, they planted, they builded; but in the day that Lot went out from Sodom it rained fire and brimstone from heaven, and destroyed them all: after the same manner shall it be in the day that the Son of man is revealed. In that day, he which shall be on the housetop, and his goods in the house, let him not go down to take them away: and let him that is in the field likewise not return back. Remember Lot's wife. Whosoever shall seek to gain his life shall lose it: but whosoever shall lose his life shall preserve it. I say unto you, In that night there shall be two men on one bed; the one shall be taken, and the other shall be left. There shall be two women grinding together; the one shall be taken, and the other shall be left. . . Where the body is, thither will the eagles also be gathered together.

Luke xviii. 1-14.
The Importunate Widow.
There was in a city a judge, which feared not God, and regarded not man: and there was a widow in that city; and she came oft unto him, saying, Avenge me of mine adversary. And he would not for a while: but afterward he said within himself, Though I fear not God, nor regard man; yet because this widow troubleth me, I will avenge her, lest she wear me out by her continual coming. . . Hear what the unrighteous judge saith. And shall not God avenge his elect, which cry to him day and night, and he is long suffering over them? I say unto you, that he will avenge them speedily. Howbeit when the Son of man cometh, shall he find faith on the earth?

Pharisee and Publican.
Two men went up into the temple to pray: the one a pharisee, and the other a publican. The Pharisee stood and prayed thus with himself, God, I thank thee, that I am not as the rest of men, extortioners, unjust, adulterers, or even as this publican. I fast twice in the week; I give tithes of all that I get. But the Publican, standing afar off, would not lift up so much as his eyes unto heaven, but smote his breast, saying, God, be merciful to me a sinner. I say unto you, This man went down to his house justified rather than the other: for every one that exalteth himself shall be humbled; but he that humbleth himself shall be exalted.

HIS ACTS.	HIS WORDS.
Perea. Matt. xix. 3, to x. 16. Mark x. 2–31. Luke xviii. 15–30. Marriages and Divorce.	. . . Have ye not read, that he which made *them* from the beginning made them male and female, and said, For this

cause shall a man leave his father and mother, and shall cleave to his wife, and the twain shall become one flesh ? So that they are no more twain, but one flesh. What therefore God hath joined together, let no man put asunder. They say unto him, Why then did Moses command to give a bill of divorcement, and to put *her* away ? He saith unto them, Moses for your hardness of heart suffered you to put away your wives: but from the beginning it hath not been so. And I say unto you, Whosoever shall put away his wife, except for fornication, and shall marry another, committeth adultery. . . . All men cannot receive this saying, but they to whom it is given. For there are eunuchs, which were so born from their mother's womb: and there were eunuchs, which were made eunuchs by men: and there are eunuchs, which made themselves eunuchs for the kingdom of heaven's sake. He that is able to receive it, let him receive it.

    Blesses Little Children. | . . . Suffer the little children, and forbid them not, to come unto me: for of such is the kingdom of heaven. . . Verily I say unto you, Whosoever shall not receive the kingdom of God as a little child, shall in no wise enter therein.

Why callest thou me good ? Why askest thou me concerning that which is good ? One there is who is good, even God. but if thou wouldest enter into life, keep the commandments. Thou shalt not kill, Thou shalt not commit adultery, Thou shalt not steal, Thou shalt not bear false witness. Honor thy father and thy mother: and, Thou shalt love thy neighbor as thyself. If thou wouldest be perfect, go, sell that thou hast and give to the poor, and thou shalt have treasure in heaven: and come follow me.

    The Rich Young Man, and Eternal Life. | . . Verily I say unto you, It is hard for a rich man to enter into the kingdom of heaven. And again I say unto you, It is easier for a camel to go through a needle's eye, than for a rich man to enter into the kingdom of God. With men this is impossible; but with God all things are possible.

HIS ACTS.	HIS WORDS.
Laborers in the Vineyard.	. . Verily I say unto you, that ye which have followed

me, in the regeneration when the Son of man shall sit on the throne of his glory, ye also shall sit upon twelve thrones, judging the twelve tribes of Israel. And every one that hath left houses, or brethren, or sisters, or father, or mother, or children, or lands, for my name's sake shall receive a hundredfold in this life with persecutions, and shall inherit eternal life. But many shall be last that are first; and first that are last. For the kingdom of heaven is like unto a man that is a householder, which went out early in the morning to hire laborers into his vineyard. And when he had agreed with the laborers for a penny a day, he sent them into his vineyard. And he went out about the third hour, and saw others standing in the marketplace idle; and to them he said, Go ye also into the vineyard, and whatsoever is right I will give you. And they went their way. Again he went out about the sixth and the ninth hour, and did likewise. And about the eleventh hour he went out, and found others standing: and he saith unto them, Why stand ye here all the day idle? They say unto him, Because no man hath hired us. He saith unto them, Go ye also into the vineyard. And when even was come, the lord of the vineyard saith unto his steward, Call the laborers, and pay them their hire, beginning from the last unto the first. And when they came that were hired about the eleventh hour, they received every man a penny. And when the first came, they supposed that they would receive more; and they likewise received every man a penny. And when they received it, they murmured against the householder, saying, These last have spent but one hour, and thou hast made them equal unto us, which have borne the burden of the day and the scorching heat. But he answered and said to one of them, Friend, I do thee no wrong: didst not thou agree with me for a penny? Take up that which is thine, and go thy way; it is my will to give unto this last even as unto thee. Is it not lawful for me to do what I will with mine own? or is thine eye evil because I am good? So the last shall be first, and the first last.

J. C.	Peræa and Jericho. Matt. xx. 17–34.	Behold, we go up to Jerusalem; and the Son of man shall
34.	Mark x. 32–52. Luke xviii. 31, to xix. 28.	be delivered unto the chief
	His Death and Resurrection.	priests and scribes; and they shall condemn him to death, and

HIS WORDS.

shall deliver him unto the Gentiles to mock, and shamefully entreat and spit upon and to scourge, and to crucify: and the third day he shall be raised up.

HIS ACTS.

Ambition. James And John Rebuked. What would ye that I should do for you. . . Ye know not what ye ask. Are ye able to drink the cup that I am about to drink? . . My cup indeed ye shall drink: but to sit on my right hand, and on my left hand, is not mine to give, but it is for them for whom it hath been prepared of my Father.

. . . Ye know that the rulers of the Gentiles lord it over them, and their great ones exercise authority over them. Not so shall it be among you: but whosoever would become great among you shall be your minister, and whosoever would be first among you shall be your servant: even as the Son of man came not to be ministered unto, but to minister, and to give his life a ransom for many.

Heals Blind Bartemeus. Visits Zacchæus. . . What will ye that I should do unto you? Receive thy sight. . . Zacchæus, make haste, and come down; for to-day I must abide at thy house. To-day is salvation come to this house, for as much as he also is a son of Abraham. For the Son of man came to seek and to save that which was lost.

Parable ten Pounds. A certain nobleman went into a far country, to receive for himself a kingdom, and to return. And he called ten servants of his, and gave them ten pounds, and said unto them, Trade ye herewith, till I come. But his citizens hated him, and sent an ambassage after him, saying, We will not that this man reign over us. And it came to pass, when he was come back again, having received the kingdom, that he commanded these servants, unto whom he had given the money, to be called to him, that he might know what they had gained by trading. And the first came before him saying, Lord, thy pound hath made ten pounds more. And he said unto him, Well done, thou good servant: because thou wast found faithful in a very little, have thou authority over ten cities. And the second came saying, Thy pound, Lord, hath made five pounds. And he said unto him also, Be thou also over five cities. And another came, say-

HIS WORDS.

ing, Lord, behold, here is thy pound, which I kept laid up in a napkin: for I feared thee, because thou art an austere man: thou takest up that thou layedst not down, and reapest that thou didst not sow. He saith unto him, Out of thine own mouth will I judge thee, thou wicked servant. Thou knewest that I am an austere man, taking up that I laid not down, and reaping that I did not sow; then wherefore gavest thou not my money into the bank, and I at my coming should have required it with interest? And he said unto them that stood by, Take away from him the pound, and give it unto him that hath the ten pounds. And they said unto him, Lord, he hath ten pounds. I say unto you, that unto every one that hath shall be given; but from him that hath not, even that which he hath shall be taken from him. Howbeit these mine enemies, which would not that I should reign over them, bring hither and slay them before me.

HIS ACTS.

Bethany.
John xi-55 to xii-11.
Sups with Lazarus.
Mary Anoints his feet, with Precious Ointment.
Judas Iscariot Complains.

. . . Suffer her to keep it against the day of my burying, for the poor ye have always with you, but me ye have not always.

Go into the village that is over against you, and straightway ye shall find an ass tied, and a colt with her whereon no man ever yet sat: loose them, and bring them unto me. And if any one say aught unto you, ye shall say, The Lord hath need of them; and straightway he will send them. Now this is come to pass, that it might be fulfilled which was spoken by the prophet, saying, Tell ye the daughter of Zion, Behold, thy King cometh unto thee, meek, and riding upon an ass, And upon a colt the foal of an ass.

Jerusalem.
Matt. xxi. 1-16.
Mark xi. 1, to xii. 12.
Luke xix. 29, to xx. 19.
John xii. 12-19.
Enters into Jerusalem.
Drives Traders from the Temple.
Heals the Lame and Blind.
Parable of Fig Tree.

. . It is written, My house shall be called a house of prayer, but ye make it a den of robbers.
. . Yea, did ye never read, Out of the mouth of babes and sucklings thou hast perfected praise?
. . Let there be no fruit from thee henceforward forever.

HIS WORDS.

. . Have faith in God. . . Verily I say unto you, if ye have faith, and doubt not, ye shall not only do what is done to the fig tree, but even if ye shall say unto this mountain, Be thou taken up and cast into the sea, it shall be done. And all things, whatsoever ye shall ask in prayer, believing, ye shall receive. And whensoever ye stand praying, forgive, if ye have aught against any one: that your Father also which is in heaven may forgive you your trespasses. . . I also will ask you one question, which if ye tell me, I likewise will tell you by what authority I do these things. The baptism of John, whence was it? answer me, from heaven or from men. . . Neither tell I you by what authority I do these things.

HIS ACTS.

Parable of two Sons. But what think ye? A man had two sons; and he came to the first, and said, Son, go work to-day in the vineyard. And he answered and said, I will not: but afterward he repented himself, and went. And he came to the second, and said likewise. And he answered and said, I go, sir: and went not. Whether of the twain did the will of his father? . . Verily I say unto you, that the publicans and the harlots go into the kingdom of God before you. For John came unto you in the way of righteousness, and ye believed him not: but the publicans and the harlots believed him: and ye when ye, saw it, did not even repent yourselves afterward, that ye might believe him.

Parable of Wicked Husbandmen. Hear another parable: There was a man that was a householder, which planted a vineyard, and set a hedge about it, and digged a winepress in it, and built a tower, and let it out to husbandmen, and went into another country. And when the season of the fruits drew near, he sent his servants to the husbandmen, to receive his fruits. And the husbandmen took his servants and beat one, and killed another, and stoned another. Again, he sent other servants more than the first: and they did unto them in like manner. But afterward he sent unto them his son, saying, They will reverence my son. But the husbandmen, when they saw the son, said among themselves, This is the heir; come, let us kill him, and take his inheritance. And they took him, and cast him forth out of the vineyard, and killed him. When therefore the lord of the vineyard shall come, what will he do unto those husband-

HIS WORDS.

men? (He will miserably destroy those miserable men, and will let out the vineyard unto other husbandmen, which shall render him the fruits in their seasons.) Did ye never read in the scriptures, The stone which the builders rejected, The same was made the head of the corner: This was from the Lord, And it is marvellous in our eyes? Therefore say I unto you, The kingdom of God shall be taken away from you, and shall be given to a nation bringing forth the fruits thereof, And he that falleth on this stone shall be broken to pieces; but on whomsoever it shall fall, it will scatter him as dust. . . I tell you that, if these shall hold their peace, the stones will cry out. (He Weeps). If thou hadst known in this day, even thou, the things which belong unto peace! But now they are hid from thine eyes. For the days shall come upon thee, when thine enemies shall cast up a bank about thee, and compass thee round, and keep thee in on every side, and shall dash thee to the ground, and thy children within thee; and they shall not leave in thee one stone upon another: because thou knowest not the time of thy visitation.

HIS ACTS.

J. C. Jerusalem.
34. Matt. xx. 1, to xxiii. 39
Mark xii. 13-44.
Luke xx. 20, to xxi. 4.
John xii. 20-50.
Marriage, King's Son.

. . The kingdom of heaven is likened unto a certain king, which made a marriage feast for his son, and sent forth his servants to call them that were bidden to the marriage feast: and they would not come. Again he sent forth other servants saying, Tell them that are bidden, Behold, I have made ready my dinner; my oxen and my fatlings are killed, and all things are ready: come to the marriage feast, But they made light of it and went their ways, one to his own farm, another to his merchandise: and the rest laid hold on his servants, and entreated them shamefully, and killed them. But the king was wroth; and he sent his armies, and destroyed those murderers and burned their city. Then saith he to his servants, The wedding is ready, but they that were bidden were not worthy. Go ye therefore unto the partings of the highways, and as many as ye shall find, bid to the marriage feast. And those servants went out into the highways and gathered together all as many as they found, both bad and good: and the wedding was filled with guests. But when the king came in to behold the guests, he saw there a man which had not on a wedding-garment: and

HIS WORDS.

he saith unto him, Friend, how camest thou in hither not having a wedding-garment? And he was speechless. Then the king said to the servants, Bind him hand and foot, and cast him out into the outer darkness; there shall be the weeping and gnashing of teeth. For many are called, but few chosen.

HIS ACTS.

Pharisees question him on tribute to Cæsar. … Why tempt ye me, ye hypocrites? Shew me the tribute money. And they brought unto him a penny. And he saith unto them, Whose is this image and superscription? Render therefore unto Cæsar the things that are Cæsar's; and unto God the things that are God's.

Sadducees on Resurrection. .. Ye do err, not knowing the scriptures, nor the power of God. The sons of this world marry and are given in marriage, but they that are accounted worthy to attain to the world and the resurrection from the dead neither marry, nor are given in marriage, for neither can they die any more; for they are equal unto the angels in heaven, and are Sons of God. But as touching the resurrection of the dead, have ye not read in the Book of Moses, in the place concerning the Bush, how God spake unto him, saying, I am the God of Abraham, and the God of Isaac, and the God of Jacob? God is not *the God* of the dead, but of the living: ye do greatly err.

A Lawyer questions. The first is, Hear, O Israel: The Lord our God, the Lord is one; and, Thou shalt love the Lord thy God with all thy heart, and with all thy soul, and with all thy mind. This is the great and first commandment. A second like *unto it* is this, Thou shalt love thy neighbor as thyself. On these two commandments hangeth the whole law and the prophets. … Thou art not far from the kingdom of God. … What think ye of the Christ? whose son is he? How say the scribes that Christ is *the son* of David? How then doth David in the Spirit call him Lord, saying,

The Lord said unto my Lord,
Sit thou on my right hand,
Till I put thine enemies underneath thy feet?

If David then calleth him Lord, how is he his son?

Denounces Pharisees. … The scribes and the Pharisees sit on Moses' seat: all

HIS WORDS.

things therefore whatsoever they bid you, *these* do and observe: but do not ye after their works; for they say, and do not, they which devour widows' houses, and for a pretence make long prayers. Yea, they bind heavy burdens and grievous to be borne, and lay them on men's shoulders: but they themselves will not move them with their finger. But all their works they do for to be seen of men: these shall receive greater comdemnation, for they make broad their phylacteries, and enlarge the borders *of their garments*, and love the chief places at feasts, and the chief seats in the synagogues, and the salutations in the marketplaces, and to be called of men, Rabbi. But be not ye called Rabbi: for one is your teacher, and all ye are brethren. And call no man your father on the earth; for one is your Father, which is in heaven. Neither be ye called masters: for one is your master, *even* the Christ. But he that is greatest among you shall be your servant. And whosoever shall exalt himself shall be humbled; and whosover shall humble himself shall be exalted.

But woe unto you, scribes and Pharisees, hypocrites! because ye shut the kingdom of heaven against men: for ye enter not in yourselves, neither suffer ye them that are entering in to enter.

Woe unto you, scribes and Pharisees, hypocrites! for ye compass sea and land to make one proselyte; and when he is become so, ye make him twofold more a son of hell than yourselves.

Woe unto you, ye blind guides, which say, Whosoever shall swear by the temple, it is nothing; but whosoever shall swear by the gold of the temple, he is a debtor. Ye fools and blind: for whether is greater, the gold, or the temple that hath sanctified the gold? And, Whosoever shall swear by the altar, it is nothing; but whosoever shall swear by the gift that is upon it, he is a debtor. Ye blind: for whether is greater, the gift, or the altar that sanctifieth the gift? He therefore that sweareth by the altar, sweareth by it, and by all things thereon. And he that sweareth by the temple, sweareth by it, and by him that dwelleth therein. And he that sweareth by the heaven, sweareth by the throne of God, and by him that sitteth thereon.

Woe unto you, scribes and Pharisees, hypocrites! for ye tithe mint and anise and cummin, and have left undone the weightier matters of the law, judgment, and mercy, and faith: but these ye ought to have done, and not to have left the other undone.

HIS WORDS.

Ye blind guides, which strain out the gnat, and swallow the camel.

Woe unto you, scribes and Pharisees, hypocrites! for ye cleanse the outside of the cup and of the platter, but within they are full from extortion and excess. Thou blind Pharisee, cleanse first the inside of the cup and of the platter, that the outside thereof may become clean also.

Woe unto you, scribes and Pharisees, hypocrites! for ye are like unto whited sepulchres, which outwardly appear beautiful, but inwardly are full of dead men's bones, and of all uncleanness. Even so ye also outwardly appear righteous unto men, but inwardly ye are full of hypocrisy and iniquity.

Woe unto you, scribes and Pharisees, hypocrites! for ye build the sepulchres of the prophets, and garnish the tombs of the righteous, and say, If we had been in the days of our fathers, we should not have been partakers with them in the blood of the prophets. Wherefore ye witness to yourselves, that ye are sons of them that slew the prophets. Fill ye up then the measure of your fathers. Ye serpents, ye offspring of vipers, how shall ye escape the judgment of hell? Therefore, behold, I send unto you prophets, and wise men, and scribes: some of them shall ye kill and crucify; and some of them shall ye scourge in your synagogues, and persecute from city to city: that upon you may come all the righteous blood shed on the earth, from the blood of Abel the righteous unto the blood of Zachariah son of Barachiah, whom ye slew between the sanctuary and the altar. Verily I say unto you, All these things shall come upon this generation.

HIS ACTS.

Laments over Jerusalem.

O Jerusalem, Jerusalem which killeth the prophets, and stoneth them that are sent unto her! how often would I have gathered thy children together, even as a hen gathereth her chickens under her wings, and ye would not! Behold, your house is left unto you desolate. For I say unto you, Ye shall not see me henceforth, till ye shall say, Blessed *is* he that cometh in the name of the Lord.

The Widow's Mite.

Verily, I say unto you, This poor widow cast in more than all they which are casting into the treasury; for they all did cast in of their superfluity: but she of her want did cast in all that she had, even all her living.

| HIS ACTS. | HIS WORDS. |

Greeks Visit Him.

. . . The hour is come, that the Son of Man should be glorified. Verily, verily, I say unto you, Except a grain of wheat fall into the earth and die, it abideth by itself alone; but if it die, it beareth much fruit. He that loveth his life loseth it; and he that hateth his life in this world shall keep it unto life eternal. If any man serve me, let him follow me; and where I am, there shall also my servant be: if any man serve me, him will the Father honor. Now is my soul troubled; and what shall I say? Father, save me from this hour. But for this cause came I unto this hour. Father, glorify thy name. (A voice out of heaven, I have both glorified it, and will glorify it again.) . . . This voice hath not come for my sake, but for your sakes. Now is the judgment of this world: now shall the prince of this world be cast out. And I, if I be lifted up from the earth, will draw all men unto myself. . . . Yet a little while is the light among you. Walk while ye have the light, that darkness overtake you not: and he that walketh in the darkness knoweth not whither he goeth. While ye have the light, believe on the light, that ye may become sons of light.

Jewish Unbelief.

. . . He that believeth on me, believeth not on me, but on him that sent me. And he that beholdeth me beholdeth him that sent me. I am come a light into the world, that whosoever believeth on me may not abide in the darkness. And if any man hear my sayings, and keep them not, I judge him not: for I came not to judge the world, but to save the world. He that rejecteth me, and receiveth not my sayings, hath one that judgeth him: the word that I spake the same shall judge him in the last day. For I spake not from myself; but the Father which sent me, he hath given me a commandment, what I should say, and what I should speak. And I know that his commandment is life eternal: the things therefore which I speak, even as the Father hath said unto me, so I speak.

Jerusalem.
Mount of Olives.
Matt. xxiv. 1, to xxv. 46
Mark xviii. 1-37.
Luke xxi. 5-36.
Predicts Persecutions.
Jerusalem's destruction.
End of Jewish Dispensation.

. . . See ye not all these great buildings? verily I say unto you, There shall not be left here one stone upon another, that shall not be thrown down.

. . . Take heed that no man lead you astray. For many

HIS ACTS.	HIS WORDS.
Christ's Final Coming. Day of Judgment.	shall come in my name, saying, I am the Christ; and shall lead

many astray. And ye shall hear of wars and rumors of wars: see that ye be not troubled: for *these things* must needs come to pass; but the end is not yet. For nation shall rise against nation, and kingdom against kingdom: and there shall be famines and pestilences and earthquakes in divers places. But all these things are the beginning of travail.

. . . But take ye heed to yourselves: for they shall deliver you up to councils and shall kill you; and in synagogues shall ye be beaten; and before governors and kings shall ye stand for my sake, for a testimony unto them. And this gospel of the kingdom must first be preached in the whole world for a testimony unto all the nations, And then shall the end come. And when they lead you *to judgment*, and deliver you up, be not anxious beforehand what ye shall speak: but whatsoever shall be given you in that hour, that speak ye: for I will give you a mouth and wisdom which all your adversaries shall not be able to withstand or gainsay, for it is not ye that speak, but the Holy Ghost. And then shall many stumble, and shall hate one another. And brother shall deliver up brother to death, and the father his child; and children shall rise up against parents, and cause them to be put to death. And many false prophets shall arise, and shall lead many astray. And because iniquity shall be multiplied, the love of the many shall wax cold. And ye shall be hated of all men for my name's sake: but he that endureth to the end the same shall be saved, and not a hair of your head shall perish. In your patience ye shall win your souls.

When therefore ye see Jerusalem encompassed with armies and the abomination of desolation, which was spoken of by Daniel the prophet, standing in the holy place where he ought not (let him that readeth understand), then let them that are in Judæa flee unto the mountains: let him that is on the housetop not go down to take out the things that are in his house: and let him that is in the field not return back to take his cloke. But woe unto them that are with child and to them that give suck in those days! And pray ye that your flight be not in the winter, neither on a sabbath: for then shall be great tribulation, such as hath not been from the beginning of the world until now, no, nor ever shall be, for these are the days of vengeance, that all things which are written may be fulfilled; for there shall be

HIS WORDS.

great distress upon the land, and wrath unto this people. And they shall fall by the edge of the sword, and shall be led captive into all the nations: and Jerusalem shall be trodden down of the Gentiles, until the times of the Gentiles be fulfilled. And except the Lord had shortened these days, no flesh would have been saved, but for the elect's sake whom he chose, those days shall be shortened.

Then if any man shall say unto you, Lo, here is the Christ, or, Here; believe *it* not. For there shall arise false Christs, and false prophets, and shall shew great signs and wonders; so as to lead astray, if possible, even the elect. But take ye heed: Behold, I have told you beforehand. If therefore they shall say unto you, Behold, he is in the wilderness; go not forth: Behold, he is in the inner chambers; believe *it* not. For as the lightning cometh forth from the east, and is seen even unto the west; so shall be the coming of the Son of man. Wheresoever the carcase is, there will the eagles be gathered together.

But immediately, after the tribulation of those days, the sun shall be darkened, and the moon shall not give her light, and the stars shall fall from heaven, and the powers of the heavens shall be shaken: and then shall appear the sign of the Son of man in heaven: and then shall all the tribes of the earth mourn in perplexity for the roaring of the sea and the billows; men fainting for fear, and for expectation of the things which are coming on the world: and they shall see the Son of man coming on the clouds of heaven with power and great glory. And he shall send forth his angels with a great sound of a trumpet, and they shall gather together his elect from the four winds, from the uttermost part of the earth to the uttermost part of heaven. But when these things begin to come to pass, look up, and lift up your heads; because your redemption draweth nigh.

Now from the fig tree learn her parable: when her branch is now become tender, and putteth forth its leaves, ye know that the summer is nigh; even so ye also, when ye see all these things, know ye that he is nigh, *even* at the doors. Verily I say unto you, This generation shall not pass away, till all these things be accomplished. Heaven and earth shall pass away, but my words shall not pass away. But of that day and hour knoweth no one, not even the angels of heaven, neither the Son, but the Father only. But take heed to yourselves, lest haply your hearts be overcharged with surfeiting, and drunkenness,

HIS WORDS.

and cares of this life, and that day come on you suddenly as a snare: for *so* shall it come upon all them that dwell on the face of all the earth. But watch ye at every season, making supplication, that ye may prevail to escape all these things that shall come to pass, and to stand before the Son of man. And as *were* the days of Noah, so shall be the coming of the Son of man. For as in those days which were before the flood they were eating and drinking, marrying and giving in marriage, until the day that Noah entered into the ark, and they knew not until the flood came and took them all away; so shall be the coming of the Son of man. Then shall two men be in the field; one is taken, and one is left: two women *shall be* grinding at the mill; one is taken, and one is left. Watch therefore: for ye know not on what day your Lord cometh. Whether at even or at midnight or at cock crowing or in the morning. But know this, that if the master of the house had known in what watch the thief was coming, he would have watched, and would not have suffered his house to be broken through. Therefore be ye also ready, lest coming suddenly he find you sleeping, and what I say unto you I say unto all, watch, for in an hour that ye think not the Son of man cometh. Who then is the faithful and wise servant, whom his lord hath set over his household, to give them their food in due season? Blessed is that servant, whom his lord when he cometh shall find so doing. Verily I say unto you, that he will set him over all that he hath. But if that evil servant shall say in his heart, My lord tarrieth; and shall begin to beat his fellow-servants, and shall eat and drink with the drunken; the lord of that servant shall come in a day when he expecteth not, and in an hour when he knoweth not, and shall cut him asunder, and appoint his portion with the hypocrites: there shall be the weeping and gnashing of teeth.

HIS ACTS.

Parables.
The Ten Virgins.

Then shall the kingdom of heaven be likened unto ten virgins, which took their lamps, and went forth to meet the bridegroom. And five of them were foolish, and five were wise. For the foolish, when they took their lamps, took no oil with them: but the wise took oil in their vessels with their lamps. Now while the bridegroom tarried, they all slumbered and slept. But at midnight there is a cry, Behold, the Bridegroom! Come ye forth to meet him. Then all those virgins arose, and trimmed

HIS WORDS.

their lamps. And the foolish said unto the wise, Give us of your oil; for our lamps are going out. But the wise answered, saying, Peradventure there will not be enough for us and you: go ye rather to them that sell, and buy for yourselves. And while they went away to buy, the bridegroom came; and they that were ready went in with him to the marriage feast: and the door was shut. Afterward come also the other virgins, saying, Lord, Lord, open to us. But he answered and said, Verily I say unto you, I know you not. Watch therefore, for ye know not the day nor the hour.

HIS ACTS.

The Five Talents.

For *it is* as *when* a man, going into another country, called his own servants, and delivered unto them his goods. And unto one he gave five talents, to another two, to another one; to each according to his several ability; and he went on his journey. Straightway he that received the five talents went and traded with them, and made other five talents. In like manner he also that *received* the two gained other two. But he that received the one went away and digged in the earth, and hid his lord's money. Now after a long time the lord of those servants cometh, and maketh a reckoning with them. And he that received the five talents came and brought other five talents, saying, Lord, thou deliveredst unto me five talents: lo, I have gained other five talents. His lord said unto him, Well done, good and faithful servant: thou hast been faithful over a few things, I will set thee over many things: enter thou into the joy of thy lord. And he also that *received* the two talents came and said, Lord, thou deliveredst unto me two talents: lo, I have gained other two talents. His lord said unto him, Well done, good and faithful servant; thou hast been faithful over a few things, I will set thee over many things: enter thou into the joy of thy lord, And he also that had received the one talent came and said, Lord, I knew thee that thou art a hard man, reaping where thou didst not sow, and gathering where thou didst not scatter: and I was afraid, and went away and hid thy talent in the earth: lo, thou hast thine own. But his lord answered and said unto him, Thou wicked and slothful servant, thou knewest that I reap where I sowed not, and gather where I did not scatter; thou oughtest therefore to have put my money to the bankers, and at my coming I should have received back mine own with interest.

HIS WORDS.

Take ye away therefore the talent from him, and give it unto him that hath the ten talents. For unto every one that hath shall be given, and he shall have abundance: but from him that hath not, even that which he hath shall be taken away. And cast ye out the unprofitable servant into the outer darkness: there shall be the weeping and gnashing of teeth.

But when the Son of man shall come in his glory, and all the angels with him, then shall he sit on the throne of his glory: and before him shall be gathered all the nations; and he shall separate them one from another, as the shepherd separateth the sheep from the goats: and he shall set the sheep on his right hand, but the goats on the left. Then shall the King say unto them on his right hand, Come, ye blessed of my Father, inherit the kingdom prepared for you from the foundation of the world: for I was an hungered, and ye gave me meat: I was thirsty, and ye gave me drink: I was a stranger, and ye took me in; naked, and ye clothed me: I was sick, and ye visited me: I was in prison, and ye came unto me. Then shall the righteous answer him, saying, Lord, when saw we thee an hungered, and fed thee? or athirst, and gave thee drink? And when saw we thee a stranger, and took thee in? or naked, and clothed thee? And when saw we thee sick, or in prison, and came unto thee? And the King shall answer and say unto them, Verily I say unto you, Inasmuch as ye did it unto one of these my brethren, *even* these least, ye did it unto me. Then shall he say also unto them on the left hand, Depart from me, ye cursed, into the eternal fire which is prepared for the devil and his angels: for I was an hungered, and ye gave me no meat: I was thirsty, and ye gave me no drink: I was a stranger, and ye took me not in; naked, and ye clothed me not; sick, and in prison, and ye visited me not. Then shall they also answer, saying, Lord, when saw we thee an hungered, or athirst, or a stranger, or naked, or sick, or in prison, and did not minister unto thee? Then shall he answer them, saying, Verily I say unto you, Inasmuch as ye did it not unto one of these least, ye did it not unto me. And these shall go away into eternal punishment: but the righteous into eternal life.

HIS ACTS.

J. C.

34.

Matt. xxvi. 1-16.
Mark xiv. 1-11.
Luke xxii. 1-6.

. . . Ye know that after two days the passover cometh, and the Son of man is delivered up to be crucified.

HIS ACTS.

John xii. 2-3.
Bethany.
The Last Supper.

HIS WORDS.

. . . Let her alone, Why trouble ye the woman? for she hath wrought a good work upon me. For ye have the poor always with you, and whensoever ye will ye can do them good, but me ye have not always. She hath done what she could; for in that she poured this ointment upon my body, she did it to prepare me for burial. Verily I say unto you, Wheresoever this gospel shall be preached in the whole world, that also which this woman hath done shall be spoken of for a memorial of her.

. . . Go into the city, and there shall meet you a man bearing a pitcher of water: follow him; and whersoever he shall enter in, say to the goodman of the house, The Master saith, Where is my guest-chamber, where I shall eat the passover with my disciples? And he will himself shew you a large upper room furnished *and* ready: and there make ready for us.

. . . With desire, I have desired to eat the passover with you before I suffer: for I say unto you, I will not eat it, until it be fulfilled in the kingdom of God. (the bread)

. . . Take ye, eat; this is my body which is given for you; this do in remembrance of me. (the wine)

Take this and divide it among yourselves: Drink ye *all* of it: for this is the new covenant in my blood which is shed for many unto remission of sins. Verily I say unto you, I will not drink henceforth of this fruit of the vine, until that day when I drink it new with you in my Father's kingdom.

(He washes Disciples' feet.) What I do thou knowest not now: but thou shalt understand hereafter. . . If I wash thee not thou hast no part with me. . . He that is bathed needeth not save to wash his feet, but is clean every whit: and ye are clean, but *not all.*

. . . Know ye what I have done to you? Ye call me, Master, and, Lord: and ye say well, for so I am. If I then, the Lord and the Master, have washed your feet, ye also ought to wash one another's feet. For I have given you an example, that ye also should do as I have done to you. Verily, verily, I say unto you, A servant is not greater than his lord; neither one that is sent greater than he that sent him. If ye know these things, blessed are ye if ye do them. I speak not of you all: I know whom I have chosen: but that the scripture may be fulfilled, He that eateth my bread lifted up his heel against me. From henceforth I tell you before it come to pass, that, when

HIS WORDS.

it is come to pass, ye may believe that I am *he*. Verily, verily, I say unto you, He that receiveth whomsoever I send receiveth me; and he that receiveth me receiveth him that sent me.

Verily I say unto you, that one of you shall betray me. Even he that eateth with me. (To John.) He it is for whom I shall dip the sop and give it him. The Son of man goeth, even as it is written of him: but woe unto that man through whom the Son of man is betrayed! good were it for that man if he had not been born. (Judas—Is it I, Rabbi?) Thou hast said: that thou doest do quickly, (Judas retires).

Now is the Son of man glorified, and God is glorified in him; and God shall glorify him in himself, and straightway shall he glorify him. Little children, yet a little while I am with you. Ye shall seek me: and as I said unto the Jews, Whither I go, ye cannot come; so now I say unto you. A new commandment I give unto you, that ye love one another; even as I have loved you, that ye also love one another. By this shall all men know that ye are my disciples, if ye have love one to another.

Whither I go, thou canst not follow me now; but thou shalt follow afterwards.

Let not your heart be troubled: ye believe in God, believe also in me. In my Father's house are many mansions; if it were not so, I would have told you; for I go to prepare a place for you. And if I go and prepare a place for you, I come again, and will receive you unto myself; that where I am, *there* ye may be also. And whither I go, ye know the way. . . . I am the way, and the truth, and the life: no one cometh unto the Father, but by me. If ye had known me, ye would have known my Father also: from henceforth ye know him, and have seen him. . . . Have I been so long time with you, and dost thou not know me, Philip? he that hath seen me hath seen the Father; how sayest thou, Shew us the Father? Believest thou not that I am in the Father, and the Father in me? The words that I say unto I speak not from myself: but the Father abiding in me doeth his works. Believe me that I am in the Father, and the Father in me: or else believe me for the very work's sake. Verily, verily, I say unto you, He that believeth on me, the works that I do shall he do also; and greater *works* than these shall he do; because I go unto the Father. And whatsoever ye shall ask in my name, that will I do, that

HIS WORDS.

the Father may be glorified in the Son. If ye shall ask me any thing in my name, that will I do. If ye love me, ye will keep my commandments. And I will pray the Father, and he shall give you another Comforter, that he may be with you for ever, *even* the Spirit of truth: whom the world cannot receive; for it beholdeth him not, neither knoweth him; ye know him; for he abideth with you, and shall be in you. I will not leave you desolate; I come unto you. Yet a little while, and the world beholdeth me no more; but ye behold me: because I live, ye shall live also. In that day ye shall know that I am in my Father, and ye in me, and I in you. He that hath my commandments, and keepeth them, he it is that loveth me: and he that loveth me shall be loved of my Father, and I will love him, and will manifest myself unto him. . . . If a man love me, he will keep my word: and my Father will love him, and we will come unto him, and make our abode with him. He that loveth me not keepeth not my words: and the word which ye hear is not mine, but the Father's who sent me.

These things have I spoken unto you, while *yet* abiding with you. But the Comforter, *even* the Holy Spirit, whom the Father will send in my name, he shall teach you all things, and bring to your remembrance all that I said unto you. Peace I leave with you; my peace I give unto you: not as the world giveth, give I unto you. Let not your heart be troubled, neither let it be fearful. Ye heard how I said to you, I go away, and I come unto you. If ye loved me, ye would have rejoiced, because I go unto the Father: for the Father is greater than I. And now I have told you before it come to pass, ye may believe. I will no more speak much with you, for the prince of the world cometh: and he hath nothing in me; but that the world may know that I love the Father, and as the Father gave me commandment, even so I do. Arise, let us go hence.

I am the true vine, and my Father is the husbandman. Every branch in me that beareth not fruit, he taketh it away: and every *branch* that beareth fruit, he cleanseth it, that it may bear more fruit. Already ye are clean because of the word which I have spoken unto you. Abide in me, and I in you. As the branch cannot bear fruit of itself, except it abide in the vine; so neither can ye, except ye abide in me. I am the vine, ye are the branches: He that abideth in me, and I in him, the same beareth much fruit: for apart from me ye can do nothing. If a

HIS WORDS.

man abide not in me, he is cast forth as a branch, and is withered; and they gather them, and cast them into the fire, and they are burned. If ye abide in me, and my words abide in you, ask whatsoever ye will, and it shall be done unto you. Herein is my Father glorified, that ye bear much fruit; and *so* shall ye be my disciples. Even as the Father hath loved me, I also have loved you: abide ye in my love. If ye keep my commandments, ye shall abide in my love; even as I have kept my Father's commandments, and abide in his love. These things have I spoken unto you, that my joy may be in you, and *that* your joy may be fulfilled. This is my commandment, that ye love one another, even as I have loved you. Greater love hath no man than this, that a man lay down his life for h s friends. Ye are my friends, if ye do the things which I command you. No longer do I call you servants; for the servant knoweth not what his lord doeth: but I have called you friends; for all things that I heard from my Father I have made known unto you. Ye did not choose me, but I chose you, and appointed you, that ye should go and bear fruit, and *that* your fruit should abide: that whatsoever ye shall ask of the Father in my name, he may give it you. These things I command you, that ye may love one another. If the world hateth you, ye know that it hath hated me before *it hated* you. If ye were of the world, the world would love its own: but because ye are not of the world, but I chose you out of the world, therefore the world hateth you. Remember the word that I said unto you, A servant is not greater than his lord. If they persecuted me, they will also persecute you; if they kept my word, they will keep yours also. But all these things will they do unto you for my name's sake, because they know not him that sent me. If I had not come and spoken unto them, they had not had sin: but now they have no excuse for their sin. He that hateth me hateth my Father also. If I had not done among them the works which none other did, they had not had sin: but now have they both seen and hated both me and my Father. But *this cometh to pass*, that the word may be fulfilled that is written in their law, They hated me without a cause. But when the Comforter is come, whom I will send unto you from the Father, *even* the Spirit of truth, which proceedeth from the Father, he shall bear witness, because ye have been with me from the beginning.

HIS WORDS.

These thing have I spoken unto you, that ye should not be made to stumble. They shall put you out of the synagogues: yea, the hour cometh, that whosoever killeth you shall think that he offereth service unto God. And these things will they do, because they have not known the Father, nor me. But these things have I spoken unto you, that when their hour is come, ye may remember them, how that I told you. And these things I said not unto you from the beginning, because I was with you. But now I go unto him that sent me; and none of you asketh me, Whither goest thou? But because I have spoken these things unto you, sorrow hath filled your heart. Nevertheless I tell you the truth; It is expedient for you that I go away: for if I go not away, the Comforter will not come unto you; but if I go, I will send him unto you. And he, when he is come, will convict the world in respect of sin, and of righteousness, and of judgment: of sin, because they believe not on me; of righteousness, because I go to the Father, and ye behold me no more; of judgment, because the prince of this world hath been judged. I have yet many things to say unto you, but ye cannot bear them now. Howbeit when he, the Spirit of truth, is come, he shall guide you into all the truth: for he shall not speak from himself; but what things soever he shall hear, *these* shall he speak: and he shall declare unto you the things that are to come. He shall glorify me: for he shall take of mine, and shall declare *it* unto you. All things whatsoever the Father hath are mine: therefore said I, that he taketh of mine, and shall declare *it* unto you. A little while, and ye behold me no more; and again a little while, and ye shall see me. . . . Do ye inquire among yourselves concerning this, that I said, A little while, and ye behold me not; and again a little while, and ye shall see me? Verily, verily, I say unto you, that ye shall weep and lament, but the world shall rejoice: ye shall be sorrowful, but your sorrow shall be turned into joy. A woman when she is in travail hath sorrow, because her hour is come: but when she is delivered of the child, she remembereth no more the anguish, for the joy that a man is born into the world. And ye therefore now have sorrow: but I will see you again, and your heart shall rejoice, and your joy no one taketh away from you. And in that day ye shall ask me nothing. Verily, verily, I say unto you, If ye shall ask anything of the Father, he will give it you in my name. Hitherto have ye asked

HIS WORDS.

nothing in my name: ask and ye shall receive, that your joy may be fulfilled.

These things have I spoken unto you in proverbs: the hour cometh, when I shall no more speak unto you in proverbs, but shall tell you plainly of the Father In that day ye shall ask in my name: and I say not unto you, that I will pray the Father for you; for the Father himself loveth you, because ye have loved me, and have believed that I came forth from the Father. I came out from the Father, and am come into the world: again, I leave the world, and go unto the Father. . . . Do ye now believe? Behold, the hour cometh, yea, is come, that ye shall be scattered, every man to his own, and shall leave me alone: and *yet* I am not alone, because the Father is with me. These things have I spoken unto you, that in me ye may have peace. In the world ye have tribulation: but be of good cheer; I have overcome the world.

. . . Father, the hour is come; glorify thy Son, that the Son may glorify thee: even as thou gavest him authority over all flesh, that whatsoever thou hast given him, to them he should give eternal life. And this is life eternal, that they should know thee the only true God, and him whom thou didst send, *even* Jesus Christ. I glorified thee on the earth, having accomplished the work which thou hast given me to do. And now, O Father, glorify thou me with thine own self with the glory which I had with thee before the world was. I manifested thy name unto the men whom thou gavest me out of the world: thine they were, and thou gavest them to me; and they have kept thy word. Now they know that all things whatsoever thou hast given me are from thee: for the words which thou gavest me I have given unto them; and they received *them*, and knew of a truth that I came forth from thee, and they believed that thou didst send me. I pray for them: I pray not for the world, but for those whom thou hast given me; for they are thine: and all things that are mine are thine, and thine are mine: and I am no more in the world, and these are in the world, and I come to thee. Holy Father, keep them in thy name which thou hast given me, that they may be one, even as we *are*. While I was with them, I kept them in thy name which thou hast given me: and I guarded them, and not one of them perished, but the son of perdition; that the scripture might be fulfilled. But now I come to thee; and these things I speak in the world, that they

HIS WORDS.

may have my joy fulfilled in themselves. I have given them thy word; and the world hated them, because they are not of the world, even as I am not of the world. I pray not that thou shouldest take them from the world, but that thou shouldest keep them from the evil *one*. They are not of the world, even as I am not of the world. Sanctify them in the truth: thy word is truth. As thou didst send me into the world, even so sent I them into the world. And for their sakes I sanctify myself, that they themselves also may be sanctified in truth. Neither for these only do I pray, but for them also that believe on me through their word; that they may all be one; even as thou, Father, *art* in me, and I in thee, that they also may be in us: that the world may believe that thou didst send me. And the glory which thou hast given me I have given unto them; that they may be one, even as we *are* one; I in them, and thou in me, that they may be perfected into one; that the world may know that thou didst send me, and lovedst them, even as thou lovedst me. Father, that which thou hast given me, I will that, where I am, they also may be with me; that they may behold my glory, which thou hast given me: for thou lovedst me before the foundation of the world. O righteous Father, the world knew thee not, but I knew thee; and these knew that thou didst send me; and I made known unto them thy name, and will make it known; that the love wherewith thou lovedst me may be in them, and I in them.

. . . The kings of the Gentiles have lordship over them; and they that have authority over them are called Benefactors. But ye *shall* not *be* so: but he that is the greater among you, let him become as the younger; and he that is chief, as he that doth serve. For whether is greater, he that sitteth at meat, or he that serveth? is not he that sitteth at meat? but I am in the midst of you as he that serveth. But ye are they which have continued with me in my temptations; and I appoint unto you a kingdom, even as my Father appointed unto me, that ye may eat and drink at my table in my kingdom; and ye shall sit on thrones judging the twelve tribes of Israel. Simon, Simon, behold, Satan asked to have you, that he might sift you as wheat: but I made supplication for thee, that thy faith fail not: and do thou, when once thou hast turned again, stablish thy brethren. Wilt thou lay down thy life for me? Verily, verily, I say unto

HIS WORDS.

thee Peter, that to-day, even this night, before the cock crow twice, thou shalt thrice deny that thou knowest me.

All ye shall be offended in me this night: for it is written, I will smite the shepherd, and the sheep of the flock shall be scattered abroad. But after I am raised up, I will go before you into Galilee. . . . When I sent you forth without purse, and wallet, and shoes, lacked ye anything? But now, he that hath a purse, let him take it, and likewise a wallet: and he that hath none, let him sell his cloke, and buy a sword. For I say unto you, that this which is written must be fulfilled in me, And he was reckoned with transgressors: for that which concerneth me hath fulfillment. (Gethsemane).

. . . (The two swords). It is enough. Sit ye here, while I go yonder and pray. . . . My soul is exceeding sorrowful, even unto death: abide ye here, and watch with me. (Falls on his face and prays). O my Father, if it be possible let this cup pass away from me: all things are possible unto thee. Nevertheless not as I will, but as thou wilt. . . . Simon, sleepest thou? could ye not watch with me one hour? watch and pray, that ye enter not into temptation: the spirit indeed is willing, but the flesh is weak.

(Again prays). O my Father, if this cannot pass away, except I drink it, thy will be done. (Again, in agony with bloody sweat). Father, if thou be willing, remove this cup from me: nevertheless not my will, but thine be done. . . . Sleep on now, and take your rest: behold, the hour is at hand, and the Son of man is betrayed into the hands of sinners. Arise, let us be going: behold he is at hand that betrayeth me.

(To the crowd). Whom seek ye? (They say Jesus). I am he. (Again). Whom seek ye? I am he. . . . I told you that I am he: if therefore ye seek me, let these go their way. . . . Judas, betrayest thou the Son of man with a kiss? . . . Friend, do that for which thou art come. (Heals Malchas' ear). Suffer ye thus far. (To Peter). Put up again thy sword into its place: for all they that take the sword shall perish with the sword. Or thinkest thou that I cannot beseech my Father, and he shall even now send me more than twelve legions of angels? How then should the scriptures be fulfilled, that thus it must be? the cup which the Father hath given me, shall I not drink it? Are ye come out as against a robber with swords and staves to seize me? I sat daily in the temple teaching, and ye took me

HIS WORDS.

not. But all this is come to pass, that the scriptures of the prophets might be fulfilled. This is your hour and the power of darkness.

(The High Priest and others). I have spoken openly to the world; I ever taught in synagogues, and in the temple, where all the Jews come together; and in secret spake I nothing. Why askest thou me? ask them that have heard me, what I spake unto them: behold, these know the things which I said. (Art thou the Christ, the Son of God?) If I tell you ye will not believe: and if I ask *you* ye will not answer, nevertheless I say unto you, *I am*: Henceforth ye shall see the Son of man sitting at the right hand of the Power of God and coming with the cloud of heaven. If I have spoken evil, bear witness of the evil; but if well, why smitest thou me?

(Pilate—Art thou king of the Jews?) Sayest thou this of thyself or did others tell it thee concerning me? . . . My kingdom is not of this world: if my kingdom were of this world then would my servants fight, that I should not be delivered to the Jews, but now is my kingdom not from hence. . . . Thou sayest that I am a king. To this end have I been born, and to this end am I come into the world, that I should bear witness unto the truth. Every one that is of the truth heareth my voice. . . . Thou wouldst have no power against me, except it were given thee from above; therefore he that delivered me unto thee hath greater sin.

. . . (On his way to Calvary). Daughters of Jerusalem, weep not for me, but weep for yourselves, and for your children. For behold, the days are coming, in which they shall say, Blessed are the barren, and the wombs that never bare, and the breasts that never gave suck. Then shall they begin to say to the mountains, Fall on us; and to the hills, Cover us. For if they do these things in the green tree, what shall be done in the dry?

(On the cross.) Father, forgive them: for they know not what they do.

(To the thief.) Verily I say unto thee. To-day shalt thou be with me in Paradise.

(To Mary.) Woman, behold thy Son.

(To John.) Behold thy mother!

. . . Eloi, Eloi, lama Sabachthani? (my God, my God, why hast thou forsaken me?)

HIS WORDS.

I thirst—it is finished—Father, unto thee I commend my spirit. . . . .

Woman, why weepest thou? whom seekest thou? Mary, All hail! Touch me not: for I am not yet ascended unto the Father: fear not, but go unto my brethren, and say to them, that they depart into Galilee and then shall they see me. I ascend unto my Father and your Father, and my God and your God.

(Emmaus.) . . . What communications are these that ye have one with another as ye walk? . . . What things? O foolish man, and slow of heart to believe on all that the prophets have spoken; Behooved it not the Christ to suffer these things, and to enter into his glory?

(Jerusalem.) Peace be unto you. (Again). Peace be unto you: *why* are ye *troubled*, and *wherefore* do reasonings arise in your heart? See my hands and my feet, that it is I myself. Handle me, and see; for a spirit hath not flesh and bones as ye behold me having. Have ye here anything to eat? (He eats.) As the Father hath sent me, even so send I you. Receive ye the Holy Ghost: whosoever sins ye retain, they are retained. . . .

(Again.) Peace be unto you. Thomas, reach hither thy finger and see my hand, and reach hither thy hand and put it into my side: and be not faithless, but believing. . . because thou hast seen me. Thou hast believed: blessed are they that have not seen and *yet* have believed.

. . . Children, have ye aught to eat? They answered him, no. And he said unto them, Cast the net on the right side of the boat, and ye shall find. Bring of the fish which ye have now taken. . . . Come and break your fast.

. . . Simon, *son* of John, lovest thou me more than these? He saith unto him, Yea, Lord; thou knowest that I love thee. . . Feed my lambs. . . . Simon, *son* of John, lovest thou me? . . . Tend my sheep. . . . Simon, *son* of John, lovest thou me? . . . Lord thou knowest, that I love thee. . . Feed my sheep. Verily, verily, I say unto thee, When thou wast young, thou girdedst thyself, and walkedst whither thou wouldest: but when thou shalt be old, thou shalt stretch forth thy hands, and another shall gird thee, and carry thee whither thou wouldest not.

. . . Follow me. (Of John). If I will that he tarry till I come, what is that to thee? follow thou me.

HIS WORDS.

. . . All authority hath been given unto me in heaven and on earth. Go ye unto all the world therefore, and preach the gospel to the whole creation, and make disciples of all the nations, baptizing them into the name of the Father and of the Son and of the Holy Ghost: teaching them to observe all things whatsoever I commanded you: and lo, I am with you alway, even unto the end of the world.

He that believeth and is baptized shall be saved; but he that disbelieveth shall be condemned. And these signs shall follow them that believe: in my name shall they cast out devils, they shall speak with new tongues: they shall take up serpents, and if they drink any deadly thing, it shall in no wise hurt them; they shall lay hands on the sick, and they shall recover.

These are my words which I spake unto you, while I was yet with you, how that all things must needs be fulfilled, which are written in the law of Moses, and the prophets, and the psalms, concerning me. . . . Thus it is written, that the Christ should suffer, and rise again from the dead the third day; and that repentance and remission of sins should be preached in his name unto all the nations, beginning from Jerusalem. Ye are witnesses of these things. And behold, I send forth the promise of my Father upon you: but tarry ye in the city, until ye be clothed with power from on high.

Depart not from Jerusalem, but wait for the promise of the Father, which ye heard from me: for John indeed baptized with water; but ye shall be baptized with the Holy Ghost not many days hence.

. . . It is not for you to know times or seasons which the Father hath set within his own authority. But ye shall receive power when the Holy Ghost is come upon you: and ye shall be my witnesses both in Jerusalem and in all Judea and Samaria and unto the utermost parts of the earth.

. . . Saul, Saul, why persecutest thou me? . . I am Jesus whom thou persecutest: but rise, and enter into the city, and it shall be told thee what thou must do. (To Ananias.) Arise, and go to the street which is called Straight, and inquire in the house of Judas for one named Saul, a man of Tarsus: for behold, he prayeth; and he hath seen a man named Ananias coming in, and laying his hands on him, that he might receive his sight. Go thy way: for he is a chosen vessel unto me, to bear my name before the Gentiles and kings, and the children

HIS WORDS.

of Israel: for I will shew him how many things he must suffer for my name's sake.

(*Revelation*)

What thou seest write in a book, and send it to the seven churches; unto Ephesus, and unto Smyrna, and unto Pergamum, and unto Thyatira, and unto Sardis, and unto Philadelphia, and unto Laodicea.

. . . Fear not; I am the first and the last, and the Living one; and I was dead, and behold, I am alive for evermore, and I have the keys of death and of Hades. Write therefore the things which thou sawest, and the things which are, and the things which shall come to pass hereafter; the mystery of the seven stars which thou sawest in my right hand, and the seven golden candlesticks. The seven stars are the angels of the seven churches: and the seven candlesticks are seven churches.

To the angel of the church in Ephesus write:—

These things saith he that holdeth the seven stars in his right hand, he that walketh in the midst of the seven golden candlesticks: I know thy works, and thy toil and patience, and that thou canst not bear evil men, and didst try them which call themselves apostles and they are not, and didst find them false; and thou hast patience and didst bear for my name's sake, and hast not grown weary. But I have *this* against thee, that thou didst leave thy first love. Remember therefore from whence thou art fallen, and repent, and do the first works, or else I come to thee, and will move thy candlestick out of its place, except thou repent. But this thou hast, that thou hatest the works of the Nicolaitans, which I also hate. He that hath an ear, let him hear what the Spirit saith to the churches. To him that overcometh, to him will I give to eat of the tree of life, which is in the Paradise of God.

And to the angel of the church in Smyrna write:—

These things saith the first and the last, which was dead, and lived *again*: I know thy tribulation, and thy poverty (but thou art rich), and the blasphemy of them which say they are Jews, and they are not, but are a synagogue of Satan. Fear not the things which thou art about to suffer: behold, the devil is about to cast some of you into prison, that ye may be tried; and ye shall have tribulation ten days. Be thou faithful unto death, and I will give thee the crown of life. He that hath an ear,

HIS WORDS.

let him hear what the Spirit saith to the churches. He that overcometh shall not be hurt of the second death.

And to the angel of the church in Pergamum write:—

These things saith he that hath the sharp two-edged sword: I know where thou dwellest, *even* where Satan's throne is: and thou holdest fast my name and didst not deny my faith, even in the days of Antipas my witness, my faithful one, who was killed among you, where Satan dwelleth. But I have a few things against thee, because thou hast there some that hold the teaching of Balaam, who taught Balak to cast a stumblingblock before the children of Israel, to eat things sacrificed to idols, and to commit fornication. So hast thou also some that hold the teaching of the Nicolaitans in like manner. Repent therefore; or else I come to thee quickly, and I will make war against them with the sword of my mouth. He that hath an ear, let him hear what the Spirit saith to the churches. To him that overcometh, to him will I give of the hidden manna, and I will give him a white stone, and upon the stone a new name written, which no one knoweth but he that receiveth it.

And to the angel of the church in Thyatira write:—

These things saith the Son of God, who hath his eyes like a flame of fire, and his feet are like unto burnished brass: I know thy works, and thy love and faith and ministry and patience, and that thy last works are more than the first. But I have *this* against thee, that thou sufferest the woman Jezebel, which calleth herself a prophetess; and she teacheth and seduceth my servants to commit fornication, and to eat things sacrified to idols. And I gave her time that she should repent, and she willeth not to repent of her fornication. Behold, I do cast her into a bed, and them that commit adultery with her into great tribulation, except they repent of her works. And I will kill her children with death; and all the churches shall know that I am he which searcheth the reins and hearts: and I will give unto each one of you according to your works. But to you I say, to the rest that are in Thyatira, as many as have not this teaching, which know not the deep things of Satan, as they say; I cast upon you none other burden. Howbeit that which ye have, hold fast till I come. And he that overcometh, and he that keepeth my works unto the end, to him will I give authority over the nations: and he shall rule them with a rod of iron, as the vessels of the potter are broken to shivers; as I also have

HIS WORDS.

received of my Father: and I will give him the morning star. He that hath an ear, let him hear what the Spirit saith to the churches.

And to the angel of the church in Sardis write:—

These things saith he that hath the seven Spirits of God, and the seven stars: I know thy works, that thou hast a name that thou livest, and thou art dead. Be thou watchful, and stablish the things that remain, which were ready to die: for I have found no works of thine fulfilled before my God. Remember therefore how thou hast received and didst hear; and keep *it*, and repent. If therefore thou shalt not watch, I will come as a thief, and thou shalt not know what hour I will come upon thee. But thou hast a few names in Sardis which did not defile their garments: and they shall walk with me in white; for they are worthy. He that overcometh shall thus be arrayed in white garments; and I will in no wise blot his name out of the book of life, and I will confess his name before my Father, and before his angels. He that hath an ear, let him hear what the Spirit saith to the churches.

And to the angel of the church in Philadelphia write:—

These things saith he that is holy, he that is true, he that hath the key of David, he that openeth, and none shall shut, and that shutteth, and none openeth: I know thy works (behold, I have set before thee a door opened, which none can shut), that thou hast a little power, and didst keep my word, and didst not deny my name. Behold, I give of the synagogue of Satan, of them which say they are Jews, and they are not, but do lie; behold, I will make them to come and worship before thy feet, and to know that I have loved thee. Because thou didst keep the word of my patience, I also will keep thee from the hour of trial, that *hour* which is to come upon the whole world, to try them that dwell upon the earth. I come quickly: hold fast that which thou hast, that no one take thy crown. He that overcometh, I will make him a pillar in the temple of my God, and he shall go out thence no more: and will write upon him the name of my God, and the name of the city of my God, the new Jerusalem, which cometh down out of heaven from my God, and mine own new name. He that hath an ear, let him hear what the Spirit saith to the churches.

And to the angel of the church in Laodicea write:—

HIS WORDS.

These things saith the Amen, the faithful and true witness, the beginning of the creation of God: I know thy works, that thou art neither cold nor hot: I would thou wert cold or hot. So because thou art lukewarm, and neither hot nor cold, I will spew thee out of my mouth. Because thou sayest, I am rich, and have gotten riches, and have need of nothing; and knowest not that thou art the wretched one and miserable and poor and blind and naked: I counsel thee to buy of me gold refined by fire, that thou mayest become rich; and white garments, that thou mayest clothe thyself, and *that* the shame of thy nakedness be not made manifest; and eyesalve to anoint thine eyes, that thou mayest see. As many as I love, I reprove and chasten: be zealous therefore, and repent. Behold, I stand at the door and knock: if any man hear my voice and open the door, I will come in to him, and will sup with him, and he with me. He that overcometh, I will give to him to sit down with me in my throne, as I also overcame, and sat down with my Father in his throne. He that hath an ear, let him hear what the Spirit saith to the churches.

. . . Come up hither, and I will shew thee the things which must come to pass hereafter.

. . . Blessed are the dead which die in the Lord from henceforth: yea, saith the Spirit, that they may rest from their labors; for their works follow with them.

. . . Come forth, my people, out of her, that ye have no fellowship with her sins, and that ye receive not of her plagues: for her sins have reached even unto heaven, and God hath remembered her iniquities. Render unto her even as she rendered, and double *unto her* the double according to her works: in the cup which she mingled, mingle unto her double. How much soever she glorified herself, and waxed wanton, so much give her of torment and mourning: for she saith in her heart, I sit a queen, and am no widow, and shall in no wise see mourning. Therefore in one day shall her plagues come, death, and mourning, and famine; and she shall be utterly burned with fire; for strong is the Lord God which judged her. And the kings of the earth, who committed fornication and lived wantonly with her, shall weep and wail over her, when they look upon the smoke of her burning, standing afar off for the fear of her torment, saying, Woe, woe, the great city, Babylon, the strong city! for in one hour is thy judgment come. And the

HIS WORDS.

merchants of the earth weep and mourn over her, for no man buyeth their merchandise any more; merchandise of gold, and silver, and precious stone, and pearls, and fine linen, and purple, and silk, and scarlet; and all thyine wood, and every vessel made of ivory, and every vessel made of most precious wood, and of brass, and iron, and marble; and cinnamon, and spice, and incense, and ointment, and frankincense, and wine, and oil, and fine flour, and wheat, and cattle, and sheep; and *merchandise* of horses and chariots and slaves; and souls of men. And the fruits which thy soul lusted after are gone from thee, and all things that were dainty and sumptuous are perished from thee, and *men* shall find them no more at all. The merchants of these things, who were made rich by her, shall stand afar off for the fear of her torment, weeping and mourning; saying, Woe, woe, the great city, she that was arrayed in fine linen and purple and scarlet, and decked with gold and precious stone and pearl! for in one hour so great riches is made desolate. And every shipmaster, and every one that saileth any whither, and mariners, and as many as gain their living by sea, stood afar off, and cried out as they looked upon the smoke of her burning, saying, What *city* is like the great city? And they cast dust on their heads, and cried, weeping and mourning, saying, Woe, woe, the great city, wherein were made rich all that had their ships in the sea by reason of her costliness! for in one hour is she made desolate. Rejoice over her, thou heaven, and ye saints, and ye apostles, and ye prophets, for God hath judged your judgment on her.

. . . Behold, I make all things new. Write: for these words are faithful and true. They are come to pass. I am the Alpha and the Omega, the beginning and the end. I will give unto him that is athirst of the fountain of the water of life feely. He that overcometh shall inherit these things; and I will be his God, and he shall be my son. But for the fearful, and unbelieving, and abominable, and murderers, and fornicators, and sorcerers, and idolaters, and all liars, their part *shall be* in the lake that burneth with fire and brimstone; which is the second death.

. . . Behold, I come quickly; and my reward is with me, to render each man according as his work is. I am the Alpha and the Omega, the first and the last, the beginning and the end. Blessed are they that wash their robes, that they may have the

HIS WORDS.

right to *come* to the tree of life, and may enter in by the gates into the city. Without are the dogs, and the sorcerers, and the fornicators, and the murderers, and the idolaters, and every one that loveth and maketh a lie.

I Jesus have sent mine angel to testify unto you these things for the churches. I am the root and the offspring of David, the bright and morning star.

www.ingramcontent.com/pod-product-compliance
Lightning Source LLC
Chambersburg PA
CBHW020307090426
42735CB00009B/1254